No matter how far you've fallen,
Love Redeems

Adam Reid

For everyone suffering in silence. May you find the courage to tell your story with your whole heart.

Lessons Overview

Author's Note - Pg. 5

Part 1: Meet Mental Health Problems who taught me...
- Lesson 1: expectations are real (and sixth best is okay). - Pg. 13
- Lesson 2: warning signs are real (and love yourself on your red days). - Pg. 19
- Lesson 3: impermanence is real (and mental illness is just a shadow). - Pg. 26
- Lesson 4: depression is real (and suicide is its closest confidant). - Pg. 33
- Lesson 5: rethinking depression is real (and we decide how powerful it is). - Pg. 40
- Lesson 6: germination is real (and it requires the right environment). - Pg. 46
- Lesson 7: anxiety is real (and how to decide if the lion is in the room with you). - Pg. 53
- Lesson 8: invisible illness is real (and sometimes the scars you can't see hurt the most). - Pg. 61

Part 2: Meet my wife, Sarah Reid, who taught me...
- Lesson 9: intimacy is real (and it isn't as scary as it seems). - Pg. 72
- Lesson 10: vulnerability is real (and tell your story with your whole heart). - Pg. 79
- Lesson 11: numbing emotions is real (and you cannot selectively numb the bad ones). - Pg. 86
- Lesson 12: ignorance is real (and it's your fault if you choose to stay ignorant). - Pg. 91
- Lesson 13: tranquility is real (and you'll never find it looking outward). - Pg. 99

Part 3: Meet the rest of my family who reminded me of what a gift it was to have known George at all.
- Lesson 14: Meet my Mom, Pat Reid, who taught me gratitude is real (and it is a choice that impacts everything in your life). - Pg. 107
- Lesson 15: Meet my uncle, Dave West, who taught me that humility is real (and there is no greater attribute). – Pg. 119

- Lesson 16: Meet my cousin, Bill "Stumpy" Marcum, who taught me that transformation is real (and it can happen whenever and wherever you decide). - Pg. 130
- Lesson 17: Meet my brother, Alan Reid, who taught me the truth is real (and what you remember becomes what happened). - Pg. 139

Part 4: Meet me, again, who learned through all of his failure…
- Lesson 18: suffering is real (and I thank God for that). - Pg. 153
- Lesson 19: self-control is real (and it is possible to overcome addiction). - Pg. 158
- Lesson 20: setbacks are real (and they are inevitable). - Pg. 167
- Lesson 21: God's love is real (and we are Barabbas). - Pg. 174
- Lesson 22: redemption is real (and it only cost everything). - Pg. 180

Part 5: Appendix
- A personal invitation - Pg. 189
- Testimonials - Pg. 189
- Bible verses used in *Love Redeems* - Pg. 191
- Sources - Pg. 191
- Acknowledgements - Pg. 191

Author's Note

Welcome to *Love Redeems*, book two in the *Love is Real Series*. Book one, *Love is Real*, details my struggles with the death of my hero and my spiral into depression, anxiety, and alcoholism. If you haven't done so already, go back and read that book. I've heard the author is awesome, super handsome, and does not at all look like a little-old-man-boy.

Less important than the author's physical appeal is that *Love is Real* lays the foundation for everything you need to know—both in terms of format and content—for *Love Redeems*.

I know you wouldn't simply choose to skip my Pulitzer Prize winning book. Well, I guess I can't say that. They haven't given me the award yet. I think they're waiting until my birthday. You know how sentimental those Pulitzer folks can be.

But maybe, even though your heart is burning with desire to read the first book, you don't have the time. Or maybe you'd just like a preview. If that's the case, check out the daily *A Real Minute* videos on the Love is Real Wellness YouTube channel. Episodes 42-72 look "Beyond the Book" by going behind the scenes for each lesson in *Love is Real*.

At least watch *If My Daddy Can Do It, I Can Do It A.R.M. Ep 71*

Even though it focuses on Lesson 24 from *Love is Real*, it does a fair job of summarizing the book as a whole in just a couple minutes. For those of you who read the book, you'll see the video clip I pulled this picture from.

It may look as though I was crying toward the end of the video, but it was allergies. My allergies always act up when I talk about trying to be more for my angel, Georgia. If you've got a little one, you probably have your allergies flare up when you think about protecting them too.

If you decide to watch one more while you're there, check out *A Highlight Reel of the Highlight of My Life A.R.M. Ep 61*. You don't need to watch this video to know anything for the series, but you might as well do it anyway to see why my allergies act up the way they do. It's a highlight video of Georgia's life.

While you are there, hit the subscribe button and ring the bell to turn on your notifications. Also, if you liked the videos, I think it's safe to say you'll enjoy the first book.

In the finale of the series, *Love > ___*, we will switch our attention to who has really mattered in my life: my students, you, and the rest of the world. Before we get to book three, you'll need to get started on book two. And we'll start with what was most real in my life for over a decade: mental health problems.

Part 1: Meet Mental Health Problems who taught me...

I've started off hot with some grammatical abnormalities. Typically, Mental Health Problems wouldn't be capitalized, and they wouldn't be a "who."

But that's the problem. We think of this epidemic as a faceless and nameless herd of illnesses. To people suffering with mental health issues, these problems are not a stranger passing unnoticed. Depression is their closest companion. Anxiety is their truest confidant. For a lot of us, our mental illness knows us better than anyone else in the world. These people know Mental Health Problems by name. They talk to them daily. They are on a first name basis.

I put this message out on Facebook:

In the Love is Real Series, I include pictures of the people who taught me the lessons for each part. For "Meet Mental Health Problems," I want pictures of you all. I want to show mental health problems don't just afflict the weak. Or the young. Or the old. Or men. Or women. Or white people. Or black people. Or introverts, extroverts, tall, short, heavy, skinny, or...

It could be anyone. Could be your best friend, your parents, your kids. Could be you. The book series is about being real and facing the truth. The truth is a lot of you have problems. And the truth is a lot of you choose not to say anything. Because you choose not to say anything, the people you love who suffer also choose not to say anything.

If you're ready to fight back, put a picture of yourself in the comments. You'll be the face of "Part 1: Meet Mental Health Problems" for Love Redeems.

That doesn't sound great, does it? Being the face of mental health problems. That's exactly why you need to be. Stop being ashamed so that other people don't have to be ashamed. I have them. I'm also smart, strong (mentally and physically), fast, dependable, funny, persistent, and a lot of other good stuff. Suffering from depression or anxiety doesn't make you less than. It makes you, you. So be you.

The following pictures are the people who were brave enough to volunteer. Mental health isn't just a face in a crowd. These pictures aren't just nameless pronouns. These are real people. These are real problems. These are pictures of Paul, Anxiety, and Ashley. They are Depression, Susan, and PTSD. They are James, Postpartum Depression, and Belle. They are Recovery.

When I originally organized and wrote this book, it started with "Meet my wife, Sarah Reid." Intimacy was the first lesson. It started light. Easy to read. Digestible. It was meant to ease the reader into the book. Let you settle in and get comfortable before getting to the hard stuff.

Well, that just isn't` the reality that a lot of people face. They don't get to ease into their day. They get smacked in the face with depression or anxiety the second they wake up. Yet they get up anyway. They go teach anyway. They take care of their baby anyway. They carry on with life like everyone else. But they're not like everyone else. They deal with the same struggles of life like the rest of the world, but they do it while also battling with themselves: fighting to get out of bed, fighting to smile, and fighting to stay alive.

Instead of starting with the easy stuff, I'm going to start with the truth. I'm going to start with how dark things can get for some people. But the book is called *Love Redeems*. That's the most beautiful thing of all.

Yes. Depression, suicide, and anxiety are real. But so is love. And love is greater than all of these. I'll start with what these people start with most days: pain. Then I can show you who they are in spite of the pain. They are teachers, musicians, pharmacists, coaches, principals, soldiers, and more. They are husbands and wives, fathers and mothers. They are thriving, successful people who just so happen to also deal with mental health issues. We used to deal with these issues in secrecy, but we're not being silent anymore. The world can judge us if it decides to. At least it'll be judging who we truly are, not the masks we wore for so long. At least we'll be living in the truth.

To redeem means to buy back or regain possession of. All of these people had lost a part of themselves to their mental health problems, but they're buying their lives back by speaking out against the silence and saying, "This is me." They're loving themselves so they can love the world.

Lifestyle change:

Lie number 1: You're supposed to have it all together
And when they ask how you're doing
Just smile and tell them, "Never better"
Lie number 2: Everybody's life is perfect except yours
So keep your messes and your wounds
And your secrets safe with you behind closed doors
Truth be told
The truth is rarely told, now
I say I'm fine, yeah I'm fine oh I'm fine, hey I'm fine but I'm not
I'm broken
And when it's out of control I say it's under control but it's not
And you know it
I don't know why it's so hard to admit it
When being honest is the only way to fix it
There's no failure, no fall
There's no sin you don't already know
So let the truth be told
...
Can I really stand here unashamed
Knowin' that your love for me won't change?
Oh God, if that's really true
Then let the truth be told
                             - *"Truth Be Told" by Matthew West*

The truth. That's what this book is about. It's what life is about.

Shame fuels mental health problems. "I am depressed, so I am weak. I have anxiety, so I am wrong. Why can't I just be like everyone else?"

Well, the truth is that there's no such thing as "like everyone else." There is no such thing as "normal." We are all unique. That's what makes us beautiful. We aren't clones marching through life. We all have something different to give the world.

Truth and shame cannot co-exist. If you live in the truth, you cannot be ashamed. You can feel guilt, but it is much different than shame. The distinction between guilt ("I made a mistake") and shame ("I am a mistake") is the line between life and death for some people.

The truth is that you are a uniquely beautiful being that was made to be you and no one else in the world. The truth is you've made mistakes and so has everyone else. The truth is Christ died for you anyway. Not in spite of those mistakes, but because of them. He died because He loves you just as you are. He already knows. He already knows all the mistakes you've made and all the mistakes you will ever make. And He loves you anyway.

While reading this part, read the truth. Think the truth. Live the truth. The truth is that you are important, worthy, and beautiful. The truth is that you are loved.

Lesson 1: expectations are real (and sixth best is okay).

Tired and afraid. Forgotten what's paid.
So I'll hide in my shame like an orphan in chains.
I ran from my promise but it's never enough
'Cause my walls and my mountains always ran out of luck
I can't do anything to deserve what He's done.
He just loves me. 'Cause He loves me.
'Cause He loves me. Just because He does.
- *"Just Because" by Judah*

[12] I know what it is to be in need, and I know what it is to have plenty. I have learned the secret of being content in any and every situation, whether well fed or hungry, whether living in plenty or in want. [13] I can do all this through him who gives me strength.
- *Philippians 4:12-13*

There is nothing so useless as doing efficiently that which should not be done at all.
- *Peter F. Drucker, educator and author*

Don't start chasing applause and acclaim. That way lies madness.
- *Ron Swanson, Parks and Recreation*

These hands could hold the world but it'll
Never be enough
Never be enough
For me
- *"Never Enough" from the Greatest Showman Soundtrack*
(Sarah and Georgia love this movie)

I graduated sixth out of 189(ish?) kids in the Clay County High School class of '03. I can't remember what brought it up, but Sarah and I were talking about it the other day. She graduated third in her class. I immediately felt the need to justify why I was "only sixth."

See, I was in third place going into senior year. The reason I fell to sixth was that I didn't take any Advanced Placement classes (which would've boosted my GPA) because I was lazy. I, like many seniors before me, exercised my right to an easy final year. Freedom.

The counselors put me in advanced classes anyway, but I made them switch me out. I would've really been ranked third too if I had wanted to. That was better. We were even now. Both third place.

13

But it wasn't good enough yet.

See, my freshman year English teacher gave me a B. She was one of those teachers who only had a couple assignments per semester that were worth a grade, so each one was super important. We spent an eternity reading *Romeo and Juliet* in class. Then, instead of taking a reading comprehension test or writing some sort of interpretative essay, we were given specialized projects related to the play. Mine was to create an entire Romeo outfit.

I was fourteen years old. I didn't know how to sew and definitely didn't care enough to learn. So my mom hired someone to help me. I wasn't absent in the process though. I went to the lady's house several days after school. The entire time she worked on it, I was there providing input about how it should look. I designed the outfit. I just didn't personally sew it together.

The true prize was that we got to present our projects to the class. While the rest of the class was bringing in their popsicle stick towers, portraits, and other model pieces, I got to stroll in wearing tights, a poofy skirt covered with ribbons, and a feather-adorned hat. When Pat Reid hires out her kid's freshman English homework, she hires the best.

In addition to having everyone laugh at me while I was in my seat, I was privileged to stand in front of the class. So I got to present all the wonders of my outfit as they gawked in amazement at how awesome I looked, I'm sure.

After I presented my red ribbon embroidery with sparkling gold trim, the teacher asked just a single question. "Did you really sew all of that?"

A simple question deserves a simple answer. So I said, "No."

I got a B. Basically, everyone else in the class got an A because "they did all of the work on their own." I'm looking at you, Salutatorian Josh Bowling. We all know you didn't have the engineering degree or the carpentry mastery required to build that popsicle castle with a fully functional drawbridge.[1]

Third? Pfff. See, my honesty gave me that B. I mean, only ranking me third in our graduating class would really be an injustice. Such admirable virtue should be rewarded an A on principle. Or maybe we could designate a grade above an A for that level of integrity? I think we can all agree I should be retroactively recognized as honorary valedictorian. Move over, Chris Yost. Actually, better yet, let's all mob together, barge into his home, and rob my valedictorian certificate from his mantle where I'm sure

---

[1] *I can call out Posh (his parents and everyone else in his life mistakenly call him Josh) because he was my very first friend in kindergarten and is still one of my best friends today.*

it's proudly displayed. I've got his address. I'll meet you all there. Tomorrow at high noon. He's got a house full of kids though, and they do gymnastics so they're strong. His wife is small but fiesty. Better bring some stakes and pitchforks just in case.

The justifications I've provided here are a joke, kind of, but the need for each of us to vindicate ourselves for our perceived shortcomings is not. "I was sixth, but here's why I wasn't higher." Instead of being proud of myself and thankful God gave me the ability to learn, my default is to diminish my achievements. I wasn't #1, so I wasn't enough.

It's not just me. It's all of us. We all want to explain away any problems or perceived shortcomings we have. In my eleven years as a teacher, I had kids talk to me about serious issues—homelessness, abuse, parents addicted to drugs or alcohol, etc. These kids understandably showed symptoms of mental health struggles.

Now, read that last sentence again. There's a word that shouldn't be in there. In fact, there is a word in that sentence that inadvertently makes it toxic to a lot of people. Read it one more time. Do you know what the word is?

The word "understandably" just innocently sneaks in there. Did you notice it when you read that sentence the first time, or did you nod your head in agreement? "Yeah, it isn't fair that some kids have to go through so much. It isn't their fault. They shouldn't have to justify themselves. I'm glad they sought out help."

What about the kids who haven't experienced tangible hardships? What about the ones in homes that aren't broken? What about the kids whose parents love them and tell them so? Isn't it just as understandable that those kids could struggle with mental health problems too?

I didn't originally hide understandably in that sentence as a subtle test for you. I was just writing the lesson.

"These kids understandably showed symptoms of mental health struggles."

My new career focuses on raising mental health awareness and ending mental health stigma, but I am still perpetuating it with that sentence. The depth of the mental health stigma doesn't stem solely from people screaming nonsense about how depression isn't real or how everybody just needs to suck it up and be tough like them. The stigma is also from "enlightened" people like me. People who care—like you.

If I say it is understandable that a person facing extreme difficulties would suffer mental health problems, then I have inadvertently stated the opposite as well. If our ticket to admitting we need help is external struggles, then kids who don't face those external struggles aren't given that ticket. We're telling the kids without a ticket that it is not understandable for them to have mental health problems. We're spouting the same nonsense. "You aren't from a broken home? Your parents aren't drug addicts? Then suck it up. Be tough. Depression isn't real for you."

These kids are scanned over when we're searching for people to help. After all, they don't need help. They've got everything under control—don't they?

I've seen mental health problems where we usually look. But where I saw mental health problems the most during my eleven years as a teacher, coach, and club sponsor is with kids who adults think don't have "real problems." And it's not even close.

Within the 3,000+ students I've worked with, those who struggle with depression or anxiety the most are the ones society says shouldn't haven't a problem: high-achieving kids. It's been the kid with straight A's. The football player. The cheerleader. The captain of the academic team. It's the valedictorian. It's the nicest kid in class. It's the kid who no parent or teacher ever checks in on because they don't have to. It's the kid who has it all together.

And they are suffocated by the fear that they'll mess up. The expectations others have for them (and that they have for themselves) become a weight that bears down on their life. It becomes a fog they wade through.

If their parents are proud because they get all A's, what happens if they get a B? If their teachers praise them for participating and answering questions, what happens if they are called on but don't know the answer? If they are complimented for always smiling and being in a good mood, what happens when they aren't in a good mood and don't feel like smiling?

These kids have an unyielding, unflinching belief that they matter only because of what they can do. They become adults who continue living by that belief. Their lives are built around the certainty that their good grades and trophies are proof that they are worthy. And the even greater certainty that if those good grades and trophies go away, then that's proof they are no longer good. Proof they are in fact bad.

While we praise them for all their accomplishments, we fail to see the struggle some of them face to reach that standard. Lots of kids are doing homework until two or three in the morning every night. Most of them are only averaging three to four hours of sleep. There are eight- and nine-year-olds with test anxiety. Many of these kids don't grow up to escape the suffocating grip of expectation. Kids from elementary school to universities are fighting the fear that they'll fail. And to them, that failure won't just represent their grade on a test. It's their grade as a person. It's their grade in life.

Their world is consumed by influences telling them they have to be more. Good isn't good enough. They have to be the best. So they work harder. They become the best. Everyone applauds them for it, but they don't applaud themselves. Their success is driven by an environment that is the perfect recipe for mental health struggles: stress, lack of sleep, rumination on the possibility of failure, fear of disappointing everyone, poor nutrition, clinging to an image they believe they have to uphold.

So tonight those kids will be awake at 3 AM again, studying. They'll cut out anything they believe wastes time: hanging out with friends, spending time with the family, taking a break to relax. They'll dedicate themselves to being the best. The best don't have time to sleep. Or eat right. Or do anything other than be the best. They can live in an environment that would destroy the mental health of a normal person, but they can do it because they are the best. Or so they think. And we allow them to think like this, but these kids aren't robots; they're people.

They live their lives showing only half of themselves to the world. They amplify their positive traits as a means of deflecting anyone's attempts to look deeper. They smile just a little bit bigger. They laugh just a little bit louder. They hug just a little firmer. They try just a little harder.

They'll be successful because their life is centered around being a success. They'll be doctors, lawyers, CEOs, and many other fancy titles.

All the while, they'll be terrified that someone may find out they are not who they pretend to be. Someone may see behind the mask to the hurt and pain hiding beneath the perfection.

And we support them in it. We tell them good job. We tell them we are proud of them. We pat them on the back as they destroy their lives.

Expectations Action Challenge
- In a broad sense, in life, what is your productivity stopping point? When is it okay to turn off work and just be a person? (Note: As a reminder, I have left space to write directly in the book for all bulleted sections in the Action Challenges. For this book to make a lasting change in your life, I highly recommend you use these journaling opportunities.)

Lifestyle change:

    This week, be intentional with your limits for yourself. You can be successful and driven but still accept that you are a human with physical and mental limitations. Create specific stopping points in your to-do list or schedule.

    Work. Work as hard as you can. Strive for greatness. Then stop working. Stop striving for greatness and just live. Trophies are great. Awards are wonderful. The truth is those goals that you're working toward won't mean anything if you have to sacrifice yourself to reach them.

Lesson 2: warning signs are real (and loving yourself on your red days).

> *Can't settle for nothing less*
> *Been trying to prove myself*
> *Since I was born*
> *— "Hate and Jealousy" by Lucero*

> [27.] *Can any one of you by worrying add a single hour to your life?*
> *— Matthew 6:27*

> [21.] *When all the people were being baptized, Jesus was baptized too. And as he was praying, heaven was opened* [22.] *and the Holy Spirit descended on him in bodily form like a dove. And a voice came from heaven: "You are my Son, whom I love; with you I am well pleased."*
> *— Luke 3:21-22*

> *Jesus is baptized in the famous story. Comes up out of the river. Remember what God does? Remember what His Father does? "I adore you, and I think you are amazing." It's right there. There's the core need. This is my beloved Son in whom I am so proud in my delight. I am proud of you, and I love you. Wow. If Jesus Christ needed that at 30 some years old, come on. If the Son of God needs it, how much more do we?*
> *— John Eldredge: Wild Life devotional, Holy Bible app*

> *So often there is such an emphasis on results that it doesn't matter how you get them.*
> *— Tony Dungy, Uncommon*

    The crippling expectations I mentioned in the previous lesson didn't start for these kids when they got to me in high school. From the earliest age, we push ourselves and others to be the best—in school, in sports, in life. I'm all for that. I think we should push our kids to be the very best they can be. I'll do my part to ensure Georgia gives everything she has to everything she pursues. I'll push her to be her best, but I have to let her know that she's loved just as much when she's at her worst.

    A lot of times this pressure is innate. Nobody ever told me I had to be my Uncle George. Nobody ever told me I had to be perfect. I made those decisions myself. I made them when I was five years old.

    In Georgia's pre-school, they didn't get grades. They just got a colored mark for their effort on the day's behavior chart. I can't remember the range of colors that correlated to each level, but I know that purple was the top of the top. Purple was a role model, an exemplary student. That's the only color I needed to know because that was the only color Georgia received.

My baby got purple every single day. Of course she did. She's a rock star. She's the daughter of Adam Reid. As such, perfection was required. Never spoken, but understood.

But one day a couple months into school, I noticed what I thought was a different colored mark on her calendar for that day. I'm colorblind, so I wasn't sure. I mean, it's Georgia. Surely I was mistaken. She is a purple kind of kid. In class and in life. Always.

I asked Georgia about it. She stared at the mark in silence for almost 30 seconds. She can see colors, but she was just as perplexed as me. How could she not be an exemplary student? Her little lip started quivering as she mulled over her failure.

She had only gotten pink that day. Pink was just "excellent job." It was only second best. She started tearing up and recounting her day. Was she bad at breakfast? No, she'd gotten her milk and sat at her desk. Was she bad at nap time? Nope, she'd had a little trouble sleeping, but she'd stayed really still and quiet with her eyes closed so no one would know she was awake.

She was genuinely confused as to how such an atrocity and slander could be brought against her good name. Second best? This wasn't something she just let slide off her shoulders. She kept coming back to it again and again throughout the day. Reliving every second. She had finished all her coloring. Stayed in the lines, even. She had listened to the teacher. She had shared her toys. She had done everything she was supposed to do, but that still hadn't been enough. Her teacher thought she was only second best that day. We live in a world so driven by achievement that anything other than the best is the worst. Any color other than purple means you are a failure. She was pink.

Don't worry though. The crisis was averted. Eventually, Georgia figured out what happened. It was so obvious. The answer was right in front of us the whole time.

She told me, "Ohhh. I know what happened. I bet my teacher's purple highlighter ran out of ink so she had to use the pink one."

Then she was better. She had really been a purple student, but her teacher's marker wasn't working. Those things happen. No big deal. Maybe she could talk to her teacher tomorrow. Give her a gentle reminder to have some highlighters in reserve for next time. We can't have the purple marker running out of ink. Finally, Georgia was okay with being second best. It was okay to be second best if first best wasn't an option. It's okay to be second best if everyone knows you should've been first.

At first, I thought this story was cute. I told my family and laughed about her creativity in coming up with that excuse. Now I see it for what it really was. I was raising my daughter to be just like me. A daughter who would have to justify only graduating in sixth place because sixth isn't first. A daughter who doesn't have the option to have bad days.

She'll be the kid who all the teachers love because she makes their lives so easy. Her work will always be completed and neat. She'll answer questions aloud in class. She's going to be the kid all of her coaches love because she follows their instructions to the letter.

Right now, Georgia is the kid everyone pats on the back for being so great. She loves animals. As of today and her being six years old, her future career is "pet-sitter." That may morph into being a vet. I have no doubt she'll succeed in that or whatever else she chooses. And people will all pat her on the back for being so great as an adult too. She'll be smart, yet personable. She'll care about everyone. She'll love everybody who walks through the doors of her business. Except maybe herself.

She's on the path so many kids head down. She's the girl who is great so often that everyone forgets to tell her it's okay not to be great sometimes. It's okay not to know the answer. It's okay not to be perfect.

People won't think it's "understandable" for her to have mental health problems. One day, that girl who is suffering but doesn't feel like she can ask for help will be my daughter. Or it may be yours. Unless we do something about it.

We shouldn't wait to fix mental health problems once they surface. Trust me, by the time anyone else sees it, those issues have been growing for a very long time. They've become a part of who the person is—the way they think, act, and feel—over their entire lifetime.

My mental health problems started at nineteen when George died, but I had begun planting the seeds when I was five or six. An oak tree doesn't grow overnight. Maybe your life hasn't bottomed out yet. See the warning signs. Stop your pain before it goes further.

We can't retroactively rebuild the lives and psyches our expectations of perfection have destroyed. It's not an individual problem. It's a societal epidemic. Tell your kids you're proud of them when they succeed. Tell your partner you're thrilled when they get their promotion. Tell your friend you're happy they're accepted into that school.

But be sure those aren't the only times you praise them. Tell them you love them on a Tuesday afternoon. Tell them you are proud of them while they watch their favorite show. Let them know they are loved just because they are loved. Maybe then your kid will actually believe you when you tell them you're proud of them even though they didn't succeed. Maybe then your partner will believe you when you say it's okay that they didn't get the promotion. Maybe then your friend will believe you when you say they're still going to do great in life even though their dream school sent them a rejection letter.

    Maybe then the people we love can still love themselves on their pink days. Even if the purple marker still has ink in it.

Warning Signs Action Challenge

For each color, describe yourself throughout those types of days. Who have you been? What have you done on those days to make you feel like that level of a person? How do you feel about yourself when you've had those kinds of days?

- Purple = role model/exemplary person

- Pink = excellent person

- Blue = good person

- Red = needs improvement

The truth is, we all experience the entire range of these days. Some days we are at our best. Some days we are at our worst. Most days we are somewhere in between. We all have days when we just don't have the motivation. Days when we aren't in good moods. Days when we aren't our best selves.
- If you are like most people, you feel the need to pretend you only have "purple days." This goes beyond just wanting to be pleasant and friendly. You can still be cordial while admitting you are having a pink kind of day (or even a blue or red). So if it isn't for the benefit of others, explain below what you feel

you gain from telling others you are having a purple day when you aren't. This isn't meant to be a slam against you. We all do it. I'm just legitimately wondering why we feel the need to.

Lifestyle change:

My mental health problems got much worse after George's death, but they had been there my whole life. Every little pain I swallowed. Every problem I ignored because I "have grit...am tough...am strong...am capable..." All those problems mounted. It wasn't George's death, the divorce, or the DUI that almost destroyed me. It was all the moments in between. I threw away so much of my life. Don't follow me into that pit.

Strive for purple every day. Work ethic is a wonderful thing. So is grit. And dependability. And success. But those are things we should strive for because we get to, not because we have to. We should feel pleasure when we obtain these things, not just relief that we didn't fail.

This week, we're going back to preschool. We're relearning what our teachers, parents, and the world forgot to tell us. I know it feels childish, but I want you to actually do this. Get four different colors. You can use my scale above or you can use different colors. At the end of the day, grade yourself by simply drawing a colored dash.

Sun.	Mon.	Tues.	Wed.	Thurs.	Fri.	Sat.

Grade yourself holistically each day on how you feel you've done. When you compare who you wanted to be that day versus who you were, what color do you get?

You are responsible for what constitutes the criteria for reaching each level. And that's the point. For some of us, we make purple unattainable. There is always more we could've done. We are never enough. We think this scale is universal, but it isn't. You can be a success in the eyes of everyone in the world, but that doesn't matter if you're a failure in your own mind.

Work for purple. Strive for it. Do everything you can to get it. Trust me. I always have and I always will. I'll push Georgia to do the same. It's okay to want to be the best. That's a great goal to have.

But you are human. Accept your limitations. Some days you are not at your best. Some days you are less than you want to be. Love yourself on those bad days with the same intensity as you should every day. Love yourself like God does: with reckless abandon.

That's the part we forget to tell each other—our students, our parents, our kids, ourselves. You are just as worthy on your pink days. You are just as beautiful on your blue days. You are just as important on your red days.

Love yourself on your red days. Only then can you truly love yourself on your purple ones.

Lesson 3: impermanence is real (and mental illness is just a shadow).

> *24. ...All people are like grass, and all their glory is like the flowers of the field; the grass withers and the flowers fall, 25. but the word of the Lord endures forever...*
> — 1 Peter 1:24

> *8. But do not forget this one thing, dear friends: With the Lord a day is like a thousand years, and a thousand years are like a day. 9. The Lord is not slow in keeping his promise, as some understand slowness. Instead he is patient with you, not wanting anyone to perish, but everyone to come to repentance. 10. But the day of the Lord will come like a thief. The heavens will disappear with a roar; the elements will be destroyed by fire, and the earth and everything done in it will be laid bare. 11. Since everything will be destroyed in this way, what kind of people ought you to be? You ought to live holy and godly lives 12. as you look forward to the day of God and speed its coming. That day will bring about the destruction of the heavens by fire, and the elements will melt in the heat. 13. But in keeping with his promise we are looking forward to a new heaven and a new earth, where righteousness dwells.*
> — 2 Peter 3:8-14

> *By contemplating the impermanence of everything in the world, we are forced to recognize that every time we do something could be the last time we do it, and this recognition can invest the things we do with a significance and intensity that would otherwise be absent. We will no longer sleepwalk through our life.*
> — William Braxton Irvine, professor of philosophy

> *11. He has set the right time for everything. He has given us a desire to know the future, but never gives us the satisfaction of fully understanding what he does. 12. So I realized that all we can do is be happy and do the best we can while we are still alive.*
> — Ecclesiastes 3:11-12

    I had constant companions for most of my life. I noticed them when I was nineteen, but they had been there much longer than that. I was so used to them being around that I didn't even notice them really. They always lurked in the background of everything I did. They were shadows following me everywhere I went. They knew things about me no one else knew.
    Once I turned nineteen, I started to recognize how pushy they were. When I woke up in the morning, they were there. When I went to

bed at night, they were still there. And even though they weren't very nice to me, they were the underlying reason for every action I took.

I didn't like them, and they made me not like myself. I asked them to leave, but they stayed.

No matter how fast or far I ran, I'd feel them breathing at my neck. So I ran harder. I was fast. I maximized my time management and productivity like no one else I have ever met. I made the most of every step and every second. My entire life was a blur. But I had to keep moving. If I moved fast enough and far enough, maybe I could finally get away from them. Maybe they'd finally get tired and stop chasing me.

(Warning: a gross example of my obsession with time management follows.) I was so consumed with never stopping that I planned out every single second of my day. I'd try to flush the toilet a few seconds early so that I'd time the end of my peeing with the last of the water draining from the toilet. This saved me the single second it would've taken me to finish peeing before I flushed.

A single second. It doesn't sound like a lot of time, but when someone is chasing you, it is. If I slowed down, they'd catch me. The more I noticed their presence, the more desperate I became to get away.

I made time management into an art in my classroom. I could legitimately write another book about maximizing instructional time. I had it worked out so that I would say my first instructions ten seconds before the bell rang to begin class. This meant students would begin the day's plans while the bell rang. This kept us from wasting all that time it took for the bell to finish ringing (about three seconds). The end of my instruction would coincide perfectly with the bell ringing to end class. Not close. Exactly. I would say the last words I had planned and the bell would ring as I was finishing my sentence.

There was no free time in my class because there was no free time in my life. It made an efficient class and an efficient life.

That may sound terrible to you reading it. It wasn't. My kids loved my class. We weren't drudging through bookwork. We were interacting and being productive. We weren't wasting time, but none of us wanted to waste time. We all actually enjoyed our time together (as much as high school kids can enjoy being in school). And we maximized that time. Every second of it. I loved them, and they loved me. But a lot of the time in the back of my mind, I was still running. Running to get away from my shadow.

If I was always on the move I could stay a step ahead. If I kept going, I could barely hear them screaming at me. I could barely make out the words they were saying. If I slowed down, they'd scream it in my face loud and clear:

"YOU WERE SUPPOSED TO BE DIFFERENT. YOU WERE SUPPOSED TO BE SPECIAL. YOU WERE SUPPOSED TO CHANGE THE WORLD. YOU WERE SUPPOSED TO BE GEORGE FOR THE WORLD. GEORGE DIED BECAUSE OF YOU. YOU TRY TO PRETEND YOU ARE HIM, BUT YOU ARE NOT. YOU ARE NOT ENOUGH. YOU ARE A FAILURE. YOU WILL LET DOWN EVERYONE YOU LOVE JUST LIKE YOU DID HIM. YOU ARE A FRAUD. YOU CAN'T…"

So I'd take off running again, and their words would fade into the background.

The only time I didn't have to run was when I was drinking. Whiskey silenced the voices. I couldn't hear them because I couldn't hear anything. The whiskey didn't just silence them; it silenced me. I drank until I was no longer there. Then I'd drink some more.

But when I quit drinking for good on July 27th, 2018, they were screaming in my face. All day. Every day. I couldn't run every single second of the day. I tried, but it was exhausting. It was impossible.

So I decided to stop running and start fighting. But they didn't fight fair. Sometimes they'd fade to the background. Sometimes they'd let me carry on a conversation with someone while they waited patiently to begin screaming again. Sometimes they just screamed at me over top of the conversation. The other person could never see or hear them. But they were all I could hear.

I never knew when the fight was going to begin. They didn't wait for the bell to ring. Sometimes they'd fight me in the morning. Sometimes at night. Sometimes they'd fight me in private. Sometimes in public.

Until I stopped running, I hadn't realized there were two shadows were chasing me, not one. They are cowards, so most of the time they teamed up on me in the fight. Sometimes they attacked me head on in situations where I could see them coming. Most of the time, they jumped me from behind. No matter how I tried to fight back, they countered my every move.

I had never known their names when I was young. I just knew they were my shadow. Eventually, I realized who they were. One was Depression. His buddy was Anxiety.

At different times, I'd have them in a headlock and think I was going to be able to strangle them to death, but they'd always slip from my grasp. They'd come back fighting even more fiercely than before. Anxiety would try to ensure my life was as miserable as possible. Depression would try to make it seem meaningless to fight back at all. They had been tightening their grip on me slowly over my entire life. Together, their plan was to spread their shadow over everything until darkness covered it all.

Their plan was to make my shadow consume me. Their plan was to steal my life.

I ran from them for so long. Having mental health problems didn't fit with the image I wanted the world to have of me. So I ran, fought, and did whatever it took for people not to know. I tried smothering them with good deeds. I could drink until they were silent. But they were always there.

Then, this beautiful redhead came into my life and taught me to live in this moment instead of rushing to the next one. She reminded me that love is real, and it is beautiful. Not in her love for me, but in her love for the world. And I didn't want to fight so much anymore. I wanted to love instead. Not just love her, but love the world. Love myself. I wanted to be what she was.

My pride of never conceding wasn't so important. I didn't want to run anymore. So I tried acceptance instead. I became a pacifist. I just stopped, turned around, and stared at my shadows.

They still show up almost every day. Who could blame them since I'm such a blast to be around? But they retreat from any social interaction with me. When I stare at them, it makes them feel uncomfortable because someone sees who they really are.

I accept they may always be there unless God decides to heal me. I accept depression. I accept anxiety. I'll continue to pray for them to be removed, but I am also content if God decides to not do so.

They're my shadow. They've been with me since I was around Georgia's age. It's okay if they always are. I was the five-year-old not permitting myself to have pink days. (Well, I guess I could've had pink days since I'm colorblind. They're all grey days to me. But you get the point.) I grew from that five-year-old to the high-school kid who had to be perfect. I was the kid people were patting on the back. I was one with all the warning signs flashing, but nobody understood them back then.

Now as a society we are beginning to understand mental health problems more clearly. They're my shadows. That's it. They're not so scary. I give them their fuel. If I decide to live my life differently, they aren't quite so strong. They're still there, but they're not so ominous or oppressing. Shining light on them makes them not be so dark. They are my reminder of my need for God. And my reminder that this is not my home.

Satan planned for them to break me. They almost did. But now I see I owe everything good in my life to them. I couldn't love so deeply if I didn't know the other side. I couldn't care so much if I didn't know how it felt to be so hopeless. I couldn't be me without them.

The obstacle is not in the way. The obstacle is the way.
- Ryan Holiday

Impermanence Action Challenge

Anxiety and depression found their true strength in my life because I thought of them as eternal truths. I had accepted that my struggles were forever. It had been so long since I felt joy that I accepted joy simply wasn't real. So much time had passed since I felt peace that I accepted there was no peace. At least not for me.

To defeat mental health problems, we have to understand that although they may be a permanent fixture in our lives, they are still impermanent in truth. I can accept that I will probably have to deal with them tomorrow while also knowing that my episode won't last forever. We have to understand the duality of their nature: they are permanent in existence but impermanent in their hold on you.

Sarah gave me the power to want to be alive in this very second instead of running toward the next moment or away from the last one. To just stop and stand still in the right now. What I noticed when I actually became present in this moment is that it doesn't last. This second eventually turns into the next second. This minute into the next. Every sunrise eventually turns into a sunset.

Nothing lasts forever. Good or bad. There may be a pause in between, but all things change. Live in the good moments and enjoy them instead of trying to cling to them so tightly that they never leave. Knowing that it will one day end should make the moment even more precious. One day it will be gone, so enjoy it more right now.

Accept the bad moments instead of running from them or pushing them away. Accept that they'll eventually fade as well.

There are eternal reasons for temporary trials.

> [17.] *For our light and momentary troubles are achieving for us an eternal glory that far outweighs them all.*
> *- 2 Corinthians 4:17*

- In *Love is Real*, we talked about Dr. Rangan Chatterjee's 3-4-5 breathing to reduce the body's stress response. As a reminder, you take a three second inhale through your nose, hold for four seconds, and exhale for five seconds. I want you to do that again here but for a different purpose. For the next five minutes, find a quiet place and practice this exercise. I want your focus to be on the breath. Your mind will wander away from the breath, but gently bring it back.

Your breath is as permanent as you. You will be breathing as long as you are alive. But each individual breath is impermanent. Every inhale becomes an exhale. For some of you, your mental health struggles are the same. They've always been there. Maybe they always will be.

But don't let their permanence in your life suffocate you. Your periods of having to deal with them are actually impermanent. Every individual mental health struggle has a beginning and an end. Face them with the assurance of their impermanence. You don't have to be afraid of them. They're just your shadow. Some days it's bright enough you barely notice them. Some days it is dark, and they seem to cast a shadow over your whole life. But live knowing the sun will come up again.

- How do you feel now? How does it feel to be so aware of this very second and the fleeting nature of time? Can you think of your mental health struggles differently if you accept that, like all things, they are impermanent?

Lifestyle change:

To be able to conquer your demons, you have to face them. Whatever you're dealing with—addiction, mental health problems, weight struggles—it all has a beginning and an end. If you believe in Christ, even death is impermanent. One day you will die, but you will rise again.

When you allow yourself to be alive in this moment, you gain more resolution in life. I was so busy running and fighting that I allowed my struggles to feel eternal. I became hopeless. Every mental health episode seemed to bleed into the next until there was never any relief. I was in a constant state of struggle because I was fixated on the big picture, not the actual moment I was living in.

But my smothering wasn't caused by an invisible blackness. It was caused by a tightened diaphragm. A tightened diaphragm didn't seem as scary as an invisible, nameless darkness looming over everything in my life. A tightened diaphragm eventually relaxes. Being mindful and present in the moment is how we become aware of the impermanent nature of all things.

Time is the most concrete thing you can give someone to show love. Time is the only truly finite resource. We only get so much of it. So this week, be aware of how you spend it. Are you lost in the past—either longing for better days or regretting past mistakes? Are you lost in the future—either planning for big dreams or dreading what is to come? Or are you alive? Are you really alive right now—in this moment?

The truth is that the past is gone and the future isn't here yet. What you have is right now. Love yourself by living in this moment. Love others by allowing them to live with you in it. Love yourself in this moment because this moment will eventually be over, and you'll never have the chance to go back to it again.

Quick quiz. What does now feel like? What does it smell like? Look like? Sound like?

Nearly every person taking that quiz had to stop what they were doing and gauge how now felt. They had to look around. Sniff the air.

Set an alarm for the next three days. Whatever time works best for you. When that alarm goes off, take the quiz again. Start reminding yourself to live in the now. Be aware of what it feels like. What it smells like. Looks like. Sounds like. Go experience what it feels like to actually be alive.

Lesson 4: depression is real (and sometimes your brain is a liar).

I keep fighting voices in my mind that say I'm not enough
Every single lie that tells me I will never measure up
Am I more than just the sum of every high and every low
Remind me once again just who I am because I need to know
You say I am loved when I can't feel a thing
You say I am strong when I think I am weak
And you say I am held when I am falling short
And when I don't belong, oh You say I am Yours
And I believe
Oh, I believe
What You say of me
I believe
— *"You Say" by Lauren Daigle*

God grant me serenity to accept the things I cannot change, courage to change the things I can, and wisdom to know the difference. Living one day at a time, enjoying one moment at a time, accepting hardship as a pathway to peace. Taking, as Jesus did, this sinful world as it is, not as I would have it. Trusting that You will make all things right if I surrender to Your will so that I may be reasonably happy in this life and supremely happy with You forever in the next. Amen.
— *"Serenity" by Reinhold Nieburh*

All this pain, I wonder if I'll ever find my way
I wonder if my life could really change, at all
All this earth, could all that is lost ever be found?
Could a garden come out from this ground, at all?
You make beautiful things
You make beautiful things out of the dust
You make beautiful things
You make beautiful things out of us
— *"Beautiful Things" by Gungor*

[26] *My flesh and my heart may fail, but God is the strength of my heart and my portion forever.*
— *Psalm 73:26*

[22] *Because of the Lord's great love we are not consumed, for his compassions never fail.*
— *Lamentations 3:22*

Sarah was my life preserver. But she was the life preserver I didn't call out for. She just snared me as I was running from my shadow.

I, like so many people, had traveled beyond the point of no return because I was never going to ask for help. No one was ever going to know. I had resolved to live the rest of my life carrying out the play I had prepared for everyone else. My script was written, and I had no intention of editing it. Sarah saved me.

Now, don't mistake that. God ultimately saved me, but Sarah was the vessel He used to help do so. What about all of those people without a Sarah in their life? What about the people who don't have someone to remind them that life is worth living?

Before I tell you what depression is, let me start by showing you why it's so important to understand depression. Because, once you're in it, you can no longer trust some of the things your brain tells you.

Depression is the leading cause of suicide, claiming an estimated one million lives a year. Those are the lives of mommies and daddies, sons and daughters, friends, co-workers, of me, of you. People don't take their life because they wake up feeling sad one day. They take their life because they are in physical and emotional anguish today. And yesterday. And the day before. And for as many days as they can remember. They know that agony will be there tomorrow. And the next day.

They lose sight of the impermanence of their struggles and believe the lie that they will be in never-ending pain. As long as they're alive anyway. So they choose to end that pain the only way they think they can.

People who commit suicide are doing what we all have done all of our lives: listening to what our mind tells us to do. But depression destroys the brain. Everything your brain tells you is a lie. Not intentionally. Your brain knows you're sick, so it is trying to take care of you. It is trying to take care of you the same way it has your whole life when you've been sick.

If you are suffering from thoughts of suicide, don't listen to your mind's lies.

When we are sick, our brain releases a signal for us to remove ourselves from others and to go into isolation. Anyone who has had the flu knows the last thing you want is to be around people. Typically, this is a beneficial adaptation to being sick. Isolating ourselves allows us the rest our bodies need to optimize recovery while also reducing the chance others in our social group will contract whatever disease is making us sick.

Our brain sends the same signal (reducing serotonin production) for depression as it does if we have the flu. But with depression, all of our normal reactions to being sick are the exact opposite of what we should do.

Everything your brain is telling you is a lie and will only worsen your symptoms.

Your brain says to isolate yourself because you may be contagious. We feel like our mere presence will hurt others. So we pull away further. Your brain is lying to you.

Your brain says to reduce activity to allow your body the rest it needs to heal. But the reduced activity actually worsens depression as it causes necessary neurotransmitter levels to continue to drop. When you are depressed, your brain says to do nothing, just lay around and rest. Your brain is lying.

The frontal cortex is the outer part of the brain that sits right behind the eyes and forehead. You can think of it as the "human part of the brain" as it is responsible for memory, emotions, impulse control, problem solving, and social interaction. It is interconnected with a little almond-shaped area deep in the brain called the amygdala which is the brain's generator of strong emotions. When the left hemisphere of the frontal cortex grows more active than the right, mood shifts in a positive direction and we experience a strong impulse to pursue our goals. On the other hand, when the left hemisphere shuts down, mood takes a sharply negative turn and we become focused on avoiding harm.

Normally, when we're sick, our brain causes a reduction in our long-term thought processing (so it reduces activity in the left hemisphere of your frontal cortex). It does this to make sure you focus on getting better. When you have the flu, you aren't focused on long-term plans. That works with the flu because eventually the flu goes away and your brain shifts back to normal.

But depression doesn't go away. Day after day after day, your brain keeps telling you that you are sick and something is wrong. Day after day, your left hemisphere is subdued. Monday, your brain is telling you long-term goals don't matter. And Tuesday. And the rest of this week. And next week. And this year. And the next. The signal never goes away. Eventually, your brain believes you are in serious danger, so it shifts into a "life or death" mode. We are trying to protect ourselves, so goals and other peripheral things decrease even further in importance. Prolonged increased cortisol levels cause memory storing locations of the frontal cortex to start shrinking and mental function—concentration, memory, attention, and abstract reasoning—to grow less efficient.

It isn't that people suffering from depression give up hope. It's that their brain is altered to the point that they cannot feel hope. The part of the brain that makes us human—makes us feel alive and connected to the world—literally shrinks. When we are depressed, we feel less than human.

I was depressed for thirteen years. Every moment in those thirteen years was impacted by my illness. When I was teaching, depression was there. When I was holding my newborn baby, depression was there. When I was with my friends and family, depression was there. When I was driving, when I was trying to go to sleep, when I was exercising, depression was there. And the whole time, my brain was telling me, "None of this matters. Nothing matters. Go lay down somewhere in a dark room and rest. You are contagious. You are going to get all of these people sick. These people are better off without you."

I wasn't choosing to feel that way. The organ that runs my thoughts was telling me that was the truth.

And no one knew. No one knew because I wouldn't tell them, and I wouldn't tell them because I was afraid. My fear wasn't necessarily in telling other people though. I wrote a book to tell the world about my depression four months after I admitted it to the first person. I didn't care about the judgment from others. I cared about the judgment from me.

The problem with depression is the word itself. We use the word depression as a synonym for sadness, or at least like a continuation of the same emotion. People think if they are really sad, then that means they are depressed. And sadness eventually goes away. So if I am tough enough and can grit through the pain for long enough, depression has to eventually go away too. Right? Meanwhile, as I grit my way through another day certain that eventually these feelings will go away, my brain continues to deteriorate, and I become less capable of rational, self-preservative thought.

Knowledge is the weapon against this ignorance.

Depression is not as simple as a "chemical imbalance." Chemicals are another example of a word vaguely used to describe something going on in the body that people don't understand. A chemical is any substance that has matter. So, yes, chemicals do cause cancer and all kinds of mysterious scary things. Chemicals also make up the book you're reading, the air you're breathing, and literally everything in the entire world. Saying something is a chemical doesn't give you any information about it because everything in the world is made of chemicals.

Instead, the neurological underpinnings of depression are astonishingly complex, involving dozens of neurotransmitters (brain chemicals), hundreds of specific brain regions, and billions of individual neurons (nerve cells). Brain pathways that register physical pain also signal emotional pain as well. These neurological pathways light up every time they detect something harmful happening to the body, and they don't clearly distinguish between physical and emotional sources. As far as the brain is concerned, the experience of depression is very much like an excruciating physical sensation that never goes away.

I recently read about a man who survived Hodgkin's lymphoma. Five years later he fought clinical depression. This time there were no obvious signs of what he was suffering. With depression, there was no exact test to verify what he was going through. No one else could see the pain he endured. He said, "If I had to choose between facing cancer again or depression again, I would take the cancer again in a heartbeat."

This is in no way meant to minimize the severity of cancer or the struggles people who face it have to endure. It is a horrific, deadly disease. I am just trying to show the isolation, the hopelessness, the confusion, and the despair that can come from depression.

Don't suffer in silence because you think you should be able to handle this on your own. Don't throw your life away. Don't believe the lies your brain is telling you that have kept you from getting help. Don't convince yourself that everybody else feels the weight of the world bearing down on them at all times too, because they don't. Don't accept that the way you feel is just how it is and how it will always be. Don't think your grit can pull you through, because it won't. Don't believe you did something to deserve this, because you didn't.

In order to re-think and defeat depression, as we will in later lessons, we have to first accept the undeniable truth that depression is real. Very, very real.

Depression Action Challenge

Depression (clinically called Major Depressive Disorder) is not just being really sad. Dr. Stephen Ilardi lays out the definition and diagnosis of depression clearly in his book, *The Depression Cure*. Diagnoses of clinical depression are made according to the criteria laid out in *Diagnostic and Statistical Manual of Mental Disorders, Fifth Edition (DSM-V)*. There are nine core diagnostic symptoms for depression. A diagnosis of depression requires at least five of these to be present most of the day, nearly every day, for two weeks or more. Also, these symptoms must cause functional impairment or severe distress. For each of these nine criteria, I want you to describe if you experience them or not. If you have recently experienced a tragic loss like the death of a loved one, then experiencing a period of depression is a perfectly normal process of coping. But if you experience five or more of these on a normal basis with no particular reason as to why, then please reach out to a medical professional. Love yourself (and the people who love you) enough to get help.

1. Depressed mood

2. Loss of interest or pleasure in nearly all activities

3. A large increase or decrease in appetite/weight

4. Insomnia or hypersomnia (greatly increased sleep)

5. Slowing of physical movements, or severe agitation

6. Intense fatigue

7. Excessive feelings of guilt or worthlessness

8. Difficulty concentrating or making decisions

9. Frequent thoughts of death, or suicidality

Lifestyle change:

Love is about showing someone their beauty, worth, and importance. The same is true for showing yourself love. How can you show yourself you are important if you don't even really know who you are?

You will need a partner for this one. For the next seven nights before you go to sleep, I want you to check in with yourself on how you have felt throughout the day. Use the nine criteria of this action challenge to guide your examination. Encourage your partner to do the same. I don't want you to share anything with each other during these seven days. Just examine yourself and gain a better understanding of your mental status. Some days will be good. Some will be bad. And, honestly, within basically every day you'll find both good and bad things.

Maybe you were already aware of your mental health issues, or maybe you have confirmed that you don't have them. Even if you don't personally need support, maybe your partner does. And even if your partner doesn't, you're still becoming a part of the solution for our society by pulling these issues out of the dark and into the light.

After those seven days, share with each other. Did you ever find yourself feeling negatively when there didn't seem to be a rational reason why you were feeling this way? If you did, repeat this lifestyle change for another week. If you find that week after week you are in a state of despair, don't just brush that aside as coincidence. Life isn't meant to be a struggle every single day. If you are not where you want to be, then take action to give yourself the mental wellness you deserve. Find the truth in your life and share that truth with others. Live the truth together.

Lesson 5: rethinking depression is real (and we decide how powerful it is).

Criticism is something we can avoid easily by saying nothing, doing nothing, and being nothing.
— *Aristotle*

I wanna set fear on fire and give dreaming a fair shot
And never give up whether anybody cares or not
— *"Gospel" by John Moreland*

A wound that goes unacknowledged and unwept cannot heal.
— *John Eldrige, Wild Life, Holy Bible app*

10. *The thief comes only to steal and kill and destroy. I came that they may have life, and have it abundantly.*
— *John 10:10*

    Yes. Depression is real. But so am I. Depression is powerful. But so am I. So are you.

    It wasn't my fault I was depressed. A variety of factors such as genetic predisposition, loss, and more led to my disease. None of that was my fault. But choosing to stay silent about it was. Choosing to fight alone because of shame and a misguided belief about self-reliance was my fault.

    Depression by itself is devastating. It doesn't need our help in destroying lives. We give depression its true strength through our reaction to it. Well, I guess it's not our reaction; it's our inaction. It's our paralysis and fear. It's our silence, misinterpretation, and judgment.

    Depression's true strength is that we let it tell us how we should fight back. Depression teaches us it's okay to fight as long as you fight alone. It's okay to resist its power as long as you resist silently.

    Our silence about the issue allows depression to fester. We provide a dark, isolated place to grow: our minds. We keep our struggles locked away so no one will know. And, in our silence, we are robbed of our energy, our sleep, our memory, our concentration, our vitality, our joy, our confidence, our sex drive, our enjoyment, and our ability to love. And often our very lives.

    But I chose those things. Depression didn't rob me of them. I handed them over willingly. Instead of admitting something as humiliating and damning as "I am depressed," I chose to let everything that mattered in life slowly drift away.

    I could've reached out and grabbed those things—love, joy, peace, faith—but that would've required admission. Admission that I needed help. Admission that I was not perfect.

So I made a choice. I chose pride over love. I chose fear over joy. I chose silence over faith. I chose my reputation over my peace.

I was afraid to admit to myself that something was wrong with my mind. It was okay to have something wrong with my body. It wasn't my fault if I broke a leg or if I got bone cancer. Could happen to anybody.

But it was not okay to have something wrong with my mind. I thought it was my fault if my brain was messed up. After all, my brain is me—right? My thoughts are who I really am—right? My thoughts are what I hide from the world. My most intimate possessions. If they're messed up, then I'm messed up.

In society's current view of depression, we have to suffer long enough for the destruction to be seen in our physical world before we admit our pain. If the pain is just in our mind—if others can't see it—then that's not real enough to warrant help. We have to put ourselves through enough torment that other people can empathize rather than condemn.

I had to struggle enough to write a book about all the hidden agony in my life. And not just one book. If I only had a single book's worth of pain, then I needed to keep quiet. I had to go through enough hell that when I sat down to write that book, it turned into three. Actually, four. It didn't all fit in the three books I billed as the *Love is Real Series*. I've had to make a fourth "continuation" book to wrap it up.

Yeah. Four books. That sounded about right. Since I could write four books about how my life fell apart, now I could speak up. I needed something people could hang their hat on that said, "Oh. I've never done that. So he must've been pretty bad off." An arrest was good. Two was better. Six was the magic number. Being hospitalized for alcohol poisoning put a ribbon on it real nicely.

Alcoholism. Six arrests. One hospitalization. There is my proof that I really did try to get better on my own. I have enough indisputable, empirical evidence to say that it really was a problem. It wasn't just being sad. It wasn't just overreacting. It was debilitating depression.

It's almost as if we have to let depression really ruin our lives before we are permitted to do anything about it. "I've struggled to get out of bed every day for a month" isn't enough. "I find no joy or meaning in life" may work if it's been at least five years. If you've had no joy or meaning for just a couple of years, then it feels as if you have to keep holding out. It hasn't gotten better for the last 700 days, but it probably will tomorrow. If you ignore it long enough, it'll go away. Once you've hit five years (or ten or twenty or your entire life), there's the evidence we can give everyone else so they can pat us on the back about our bravery when we reach out for help.

It's a combination of my fault and yours. It's everyone. It's me wanting to be strong and you wanting me to be strong. It's both of us believing that ignoring our problems is a component of strength. It's us applauding our successes and hiding our failures.

I already destroyed my life. Thankfully, I've been able to rebuild it. There are a lot of people out there still in the shambles of the life they should've had. Could've had. If only they had been willing to speak up and get help for their mental health problems.

But we can still save them. We can keep them from throwing the rest of their life away. We've all lived in a world too long that says you're weak if you ask for help. We can go tell them it is okay for them to be depressed. It doesn't mean you're flawed or broken. You don't have to swallow all of your pain just because other people don't think you should have it. You don't have to throw everything good in your life away before you get help. Don't permanently damage your brain with addiction. Don't destroy your relationships by pushing everyone away. Don't throw away your physical health by no longer caring about yourself or the world. Don't be less than you are because you are trying to be what someone else says you should be. You don't have to destroy all your gifts. Please don't mock all your blessings.

Enough. Enough of this allure of what we perceive to be strength. Enough of you perpetuating this stigma in your silence. Enough of me perpetuating the stigma because I lived it. I played the starring role.

You don't have to buy the ticket to recovery with years of pain. You can find the solution now. You can fix the problem in its earliest stages. You don't have to be shattered to get help. It's okay if the world thinks you have it all. They don't live your life. They don't feel what you feel. You can reach out for help. You don't need six arrests. You don't need to be hospitalized. You don't have to live fifteen years of misery to look back on yourself today and decide you should've gotten help.

Don't wait until your life is in shambles to go public with your pain. Get help now. Get it before you throw your life away. And live the life of joy God has planned for you.

Rethinking Depression Action Challenge

We are at a point in history where we will define depression. Not only what depression is, but how we deal with it. We will decide if depression continues to rob over a million lives through suicide or if we stop it before it gets strong enough to do so.

Time for some real talk. It's not your fault you have depression. You may have been genetically predisposed for it. You could have had no more control over your depression than you did the color of your hair, how tall you are, or whether you can roll your tongue or not.

But if you knowingly choose to fight alone, then you are choosing to lose. It's that simple. I don't even blame you for trying to though. Everything and everyone is telling you that is the thing to do.

Society applauds self-reliance and inner strength. Your brain is telling you to remove yourself from others so you can heal. Well, both are wrong. It doesn't take strength to keep quiet; it takes weakness. It doesn't take bravery to fight alone; it takes cowardice to mold your life to what others say it should be.

The symptoms of depression are intensified by rumination, social isolation, self-deprecation, shame, worry, lack of sleep, etc. In other words, every single characteristic associated with secrecy is scientifically proven to fuel mental health symptoms.

- Option 1: You keep quiet just like you did yesterday, the day before, and countless days before that. You believe your work ethic is enough. Or your inner strength. Or you accept those are both lies, but you still choose to remain silent out of pride or fear. You continue ignoring the truth that you need help.
    - You know what that life leads to. Tomorrow, your alarm goes off, and you lay in bed struggling to find a reason to get up. You spend time with the people you love. At least, you know you love them in a practical sense. But you feel nothing. Not emotionally anyway. You are ashamed because you are empty when you know you should be full. Your life lacks purpose and joy.

- Option 2: Take control of your life. Refuse to believe that this is all life has to offer. Take action. Refuse to feel ashamed. Stop mimicking strength and be strong enough to say you are sometimes weak. Stop imitating bravery and have the courage to take a step forward out of the crowd. No matter how small it is; it's still movement. A small step is moving away from the darkness and emptiness you've chosen to stay in for so long.
    - You've chosen option 1 your whole life. It hasn't worked. Let's try option 2. If it doesn't work out, you can always go back to option 1. You can always quit trying.
- Make a list of something you are willing to do today. Then tomorrow. And then the next day. Plan out seven days of action below.
    - Talk to a friend. Schedule an appointment with a therapist. Start exercising. Start eating better. Go back to the start of this book and actually do all of the Action Challenges/Lifestyle Changes instead of just reading them. Anything. Just try to get better.

Today	
Tomorrow	
Day 3	

Day 4	
Day 5	
Day 6	
Day 7	

Lifestyle change:

I had you carry out your actions for a week because one decision doesn't defeat depression. It isn't as simple as flipping a switch and poof, it's gone.

But step one is ridding yourself of the silence, secrecy, and judgment. God made you, you.

It's a tall mountain I'm asking you to climb. You won't get up it without taking a step.

Now, instead of just writing down seven days of action and leaving them in a book, go do them. You already made the plan for your lifestyle change above. Take that action out of this book and put it into the world.

Lesson 6: germination is real (and it requires the right environment).

²⁵ "Therefore I tell you, do not worry about your life, what you will eat or drink; or about your body, what you will wear. Is not life more than food, and the body more than clothes? ²⁶ Look at the birds of the air; they do not sow or reap or store away in barns, and yet your heavenly Father feeds them. Are you not much more valuable than they?
- Matthew 6:25-26

Sarah and I got married in Yosemite. While there, we went on a hike and came across some giant sequoia trees that were almost 300 feet tall. We walked through tunnels that were cut into them.

It's hard to imagine that the behemoth of a tree was once a fragile seed I could've held in my hand. It was a seed that could've been crushed quite easily. But it wasn't crushed. And today that seed is responsible for one of the oldest and largest living things on planet Earth.

A lot of steps took place between that small seed becoming that giant tree. Over 3,000 years ago, the seed fell on the ground. But planting a seed doesn't mean a tree is coming. Lots of factors had to be just right for it to ever grow—proper soil, sunlight, lack of competition for resources, etc. In fact, that seed may have laid silently dormant for years, decades even. For most seeds, the signal they're waiting on is water. Then, when water comes, the seed that lay inactive for years will germinate by bursting out of its protective seed casing. At that point, the competition for life begins. It begins growing its roots deep into the Earth, and its shoot breaks the soil for all the world to see.

When the tree begins growth and emerges from the soil, it is easy to simply look to the rain as the cause of its emergence. Yes, the rain triggered the growth, but that was just one of many factors that led to germination. The fact that it was the final stimulus doesn't mean it was the only one.

When anxiety breaks the surface in our lives, we start examining the immediate circumstances in that moment to explain the problem: *"Okay, this situation happened and then I had a panic attack. So I need to not allow that situation to happen anymore."*

But we've got it all wrong. We see the giant sequoia of struggle, and we start trying to hack it down. But at one point our mental health struggles were just a seed. A seed that was not destined to grow. A seed that could've been easily crushed. It lay silently dormant, waiting for just the right factors to trigger its germination.

Just as depression and sadness are not emotions on the same continuum, anxiety isn't just an extreme variation of worry. Everyone worries. Not everyone has anxiety. But worry is a factor that can help anxiety germinate. Most people worry for a bit and then move on. But people who suffer from anxiety nurture the seed they've planted.

Anxiety is as old as humans. I believe several people in the Bible exhibited symptoms of mental health disorders. Many of David's Psalms speak for people struggling with mental health disorders. His honest expressions of despair to God and faith that God can move are models for us to follow. But he's not the only one.

> [38] *As Jesus and his disciples were on their way, he came to a village where a woman named Martha opened her home to him.* [39] *She had a sister called Mary, who sat at the Lord's feet listening to what he said.* [40] *But Martha was distracted by all the preparations that had to be made. She came to him and asked, "Lord, don't you care that my sister has left me to do the work by myself? Tell her to help me!"* [41] *"Martha, Martha," the Lord answered, "you are worried and upset about many things,* [42] *but few things are needed—or indeed only one. Mary has chosen what is better, and it will not be taken away from her."*
>
> *- Luke 10:38-42*

Mary sat at the feet of Jesus and shared intimate time with him. Martha worked for Jesus.

Most of us can relate to Martha as we believe there's merit in working for everything we get. There's honor in earning what's yours. And as such, work begins to consume our lives.

I am Martha, obsessed with working to control everything and make sure it is just right. Just right for me. Just right for the world. Just right for Jesus.

I believe it very likely that Martha struggled with anxiety. Even if Martha had been able to force herself by sheer willpower to slow down and sit at Jesus' feet, her anxiety would've only been amplified. Her thoughts wouldn't have been with the Messiah. They would've been with everything she should be doing while she "wasted time" just sitting there. She, like many of us, seemed to live in a perpetual state of worry. Worry while she worked. Worry while she spoke. Worry while she lived. I am Martha, and I believe most other people are too. The more we control, the less can go wrong.

It's great to work for others and give of yourself. But it's easy to become fixated on what we do and lose track of why we're doing it. We give of ourselves because we get to, not because we have to. Jesus asks for us to be Mary. He doesn't ask us to work. He asks us to love. Love when you're working. Love when you're not. Cherish your time with Him, with your loved ones, and with yourself. Mary was worshipping Jesus by sitting there. But to take it one step further, I believe when Mary got up and worked, she would've been working in a way that honored God too. Along with the disciple John—who has the confidence to call himself the "beloved disciple"—I think Mary was probably the most emotionally and mentally attuned person to Christ on Earth.

It wasn't because of what she did, but why she did it. She lived each moment in the certainty that Jesus is Lord. Her actions were driven accordingly.

For those of us who face anxiety, the worry never goes away. Even at the feet of Jesus, our mind is on the worry. We water it with rumination. We turn the worry over and over and over in our minds. We become fixated on the issue until it drowns out everything else in our world. A snowflake of worry builds into an avalanche of anxiety.

Watching a movie—*"I can't believe I said 'peace' at the end of my job interview. I mean, come on."* Driving to class—*"The interview was going well. Wasn't it? They laughed at some of the little jokes I had thrown in. I was trying to act natural."* Eating dinner—*"That was so unprofessional. They're never going to hire me now. I can't believe I did this. They probably laughed at me when I left. Probably told all their friends who are laughing at me now."* Trying to go to sleep—*"I'm never going to get a job. I've wasted all my time and money on college."*

And it's not just worrying. With worry alone, anxiety still doesn't have the environment to grow. We fertilize the worry with self-deprecation.

"I suck. I cannot believe I screwed up that job interview so badly. I am worthless. What is wrong with me? Why can't I do anything right? I'm not who everyone thinks I am. I am fake. I am an imposter. No one loves me."

Did that seem very helpful to you? Probably not. So, why is this how we talk to ourselves after we make a mistake? If it would be wrong of me to speak like that to you or for you to speak like that to someone else, why is it okay to do it to yourself? We don't talk to our neighbor in that manner and follow it up with, *"Now that we have those facts straight, go do better next time. You're welcome for the pep talk. Good luck. And, so help me God, you better not screw up again or next time I won't be so nice."*

We are unflinchingly critical of ourselves and allow no room for mistakes or weakness. We set impossible standards of perfection and chastise ourselves relentlessly whenever we fail to live up to them.

I gave myself a variation of this pep talk my whole adult life. Except I wasn't kind enough to include good luck at the end. When I didn't mess up and when I did achieve great things, I continued with the thought process. *"Okay? I was supposed to do good, and I did. I should be the best. So, way to go. I did what I was supposed to do. What am I waiting on? There's another job to be done. Get going. I'm wasting time."*

All the time these thoughts whirl in our heads, we just keep smiling on the outside. I kept teaching. I kept running. I kept living.

By the time we see the seed of worry germinate as anxiety, it's been growing for quite some time. It's been nurtured by our thoughts and lifestyle for years. Its roots have penetrated deep into our psyches. Its tendrils have grown over so much of our inner selves that we are completely hidden beneath them.

The key to combating anxiety isn't chopping down a 300-foot sequoia. It's crushing a small seed. It isn't in a single retroactive action but in a proactive mindset.

My favorite television show character (Michael Scott) on my favorite television show (*The Office*) shows the mindset we need. Michael had instituted "Movie Monday." Pam lays out the scenario pretty well by saying, *"Movie Monday started with training videos, but we went through those pretty fast. Then we watched a medical video. Since then, it's been half hour installments of various movies, with the exception of an episode of Entourage, which Michael made us watch six times."*

On this particular day, Michael has decided that the only cure for the "Monday blues" was *Varsity Blues*. His boss, Jan, arrives unexpectedly and is less than pleased to see the entire office watching a movie in the conference room. Michael explains to her that Movie Monday, in fact, increases productivity, leading to this exchange:

> *Jan: How would a movie increase productivity, Michael? How on earth would it do that?*
>
> *Michael: People work faster after...*
>
> *Jan: Magically?*
>
> *Michael: No... they have to... to make up for the time they lost watching the movie.*

Perhaps watching movies at work every week is not the best practice. Admittedly, he's a terrible employee who's wasting tons of time while the whole office is about to be downsized.

But it isn't the action I'm highlighting. It's the mindset. Michael simply believes everything is going to work itself out. He can enjoy now because he's not worried about five seconds ago or five seconds from now. He lives in the moment.

This lackadaisical attitude toward work is not what I'm promoting. In the same breath, it shouldn't be a badge of honor that I worked eighty hours a week as a teacher. But it was. I didn't get paid for eighty. I got paid for forty. I chose to work double that. For several years. Some of that was because I was going to make my classroom the best it could be for my students regardless of the time it took me to do so. The other part was that I was proud of working so much. Proud of honestly wasting my life doing extra work that ultimately didn't improve my class when I should've been caring more about things that actually mattered—like myself.

> [34.] *So do not worry about tomorrow, for tomorrow will bring worries of its own. Today's trouble is enough for today.*
> - Matthew 6:34

Michael simply had the belief that things would just work themselves out. If you look back over your life, 99% of the time, things do. They get worked out. One way or another. And all of the worrying was for nothing. Even if they don't get worked out, the worry wouldn't have prevented the disaster anyway.

It's not just worrying about work. It's worrying about life. If I'm an athlete, I don't have to be defined by my performance in the game. If I'm a writer, I don't have to be defined by the success of my books. If I'm an artist, I don't have to be defined by other people's interpretation of my work.

Michael isn't worried about tomorrow. He isn't worried about losing his job. He's not even worried about the fact that James Van Der Beek looks like he's 45 years old but is playing high school football. He's just living life. And he's enjoying doing so.

Germination Action Challenge

I don't have to worry about Georgia being ashamed of who she is when she's older. I've made it a point to have her accept herself on her bad days as well as her good ones. Hopefully, I've done enough to let her know that if she does end up suffering from mental health problems, it doesn't make her less than. It just makes her, her. She won't follow in my footsteps toward self-destruction.

But that's typical. Whatever problems we struggle with, we are hypersensitive to preventing those issues for our children. Well, guess what. While I'm focused on her mental health, I'm forgetting something else. Georgia will grow up with issues of her own and the cycle will repeat itself. She'll try to save her children from whatever struggles she faced while letting other problems slip beneath her notice.

That's life. It's impossible to prevent every struggle. We can't remove every obstacle from our children's lives or our own. If I could save her from all problems, I'd also be robbing her of developing her inner strength. If I could plan out a disaster free life for her, I would deprive her of the beauty of spontaneity and wonder in the world.

- I've pulled five segments from a personal file I have saved with Bible verses, quotes, and prayers to help me remain on track with the mindset I need to defeat my anxiety. I want you to read each of them aloud, and then choose one to write out in the space provided.

#1 - Lord, help me to see how much I lose when I lose you. My perspective on my life and all of life gets distorted when I don't make space for you, obscuring your love for me. Help me to search for you every day of my life.

#2 - Who am I going to be today? How will I choose to open myself to God's presence in order to be who I want to be?

#3 - Grant me courage, Lord, to do today what you have given me to do, to say what you have given me to say, and to become who you have called me to become.

#4 - At the gates of Heaven, I won't be asked why I wasn't Moses or David. I'll be asked why I wasn't me.

#5 - Your will be done. No more. No less. Nothing else.

<u>Lifestyle change:</u>
    Improve your mental health by starting at the source. Change your default mindset. We have to be able to let go. Let go of control. Let go of worry. Let go of others' perceptions of us. Let go of all the things we cannot change. Stop grasping at perfection and who you think you should be. Be who you are. Who God made you to be.
    This week, every day I want you to start each morning by saying aloud the quote from above you chose to write down. Do it before you get out of bed. Start your day off with it before your morning coffee, brushing your teeth, or anything else.
    Then, before you turn the lights out to go to sleep, say it again. Bookend your day with the reminder that you don't have to wait until the tree of anxiety anchors itself in your life to try to uproot it. If you never water the seed, the tree will never grow.

Lesson 7: anxiety is real (and how to decide if the lion is in the room with you).

7. Cast all your anxiety on him, because he cares for you.
- 1 Peter 5:7

It's the weight of the world
But it's nothing at all
Light as a prayer, and then I feel myself fall
You got to give me a minute
Because I'm way down in it
And I can't breathe so I can't speak
I want to be strong and steady, always ready
Now, I feel so small, I feel so weak
Anxiety
How do you always get the best of me?
- "Anxiety" by Jason Isbell and the 400 Unit

Even though there are many other mental illnesses, I've focused on depression and anxiety because those are the two I've faced. I dealt with severe depression for thirteen years. Although I have found successful coping mechanisms, I still have days when I struggle. I fought anxiety for a much shorter time frame (about two years), but the damage it did to my life may have been even more severe.

Some people experience anxiety in extreme, nearly debilitating rushes (anxiety attacks) in response to a trigger. My anxiety was different. It gradually built in the days following my arrest as the facts of my situation set in.

- I had just started teaching at a new school.
- I only knew two or three people's names in the whole school.
- No one knew much of anything about me except that I was the new biology teacher.
- I was arrested for a DUI six days before school started.
- I had been arrested several times before for alcohol related offenses.

If I had still been at Madison Central High School, I would've had years of good deeds to balance the scales of my mistake. I would've had countless character references.

But I wasn't. I was in a place where I knew no one and no one knew me. If they found out about my arrest, the facts were pretty clear: this guy has an alcohol problem and is not fit to be a teacher.

If I had lost my job, Georgia was going to lose her home. I deserved all of this. She didn't. I threw my life away. She didn't. The divorce was as amicable as any divorce could possibly be. My ex-wife and I have always put Georgia first and maintain a friendly relationship.

Still, the divorce had been hard on Georgia. She had turned three years old less than a month before. She didn't know how to express her struggles. But the bedsheets that began to be wet again after she hadn't had any accidents in months told me everything I needed to know. My daughter was struggling. And it was my fault. I had failed her.

My anxiety steadily grew over those first few days as my throat seemed to slowly tighten and weight seemed to pile on my chest. Just when I thought it would get to the point where I physically could not breathe or speak, it plateaued. It stopped just before the point of shutting down my ability to function altogether.

And there it stayed for about two years. Every day. Every second of every day. Every single breath was shallow. Every instant felt like I might gag on my tongue. Anxiety broke me not only mentally but physically as well. My internal struggles manifested themselves through severe back pain; skin rashes; and joint pain in my feet, hands, knees, and hips.

I went to a physical therapist for about six months for the acute back, hip, and knee pain. We never seemed to be able to make any progress on reducing the pain. I got x-rays and medical tests. I feared I had cancer spreading to all of these different areas, destroying my body in one clean sweep. But every test came up negative. Every x-ray was fine.

A doctor determined I must have an autoimmune disorder that was causing arthritis and psoriasis. I was prescribed Humira, one of the strongest and thus most dangerous medicines on the market. Humira lowers immune system functioning to prevent the body from attacking itself. But this also made me more susceptible to infections and other potentially deadly diseases due to my suppressed immune system.

And it didn't help. I still had pain. I still had rashes. I still couldn't breathe. I still couldn't swallow.

That's because I didn't have an autoimmune disorder. Not in the way I was diagnosed anyway. But my body was attacking itself. It's just that the attack was from my mind. It was from my anxiety.

The symptoms never went away because the shame never went away. More shame piled on every day I had to get a ride to work. Every time I had to carry Georgia's car seat into school reminded me of my failures as a father. I lived with the constant crippling shame of who I was.

I had been able to endure depression for so long because I was able to smother it with alcohol. I had a release. Now I had nothing to help me run away.

I tried to face anxiety like I did everything else in my life. I fought it. I mean, come on. I was super tough. I was Doc Holliday. A renegade too rugged to back down. Too resilient to need anyone else's help. If my mind wanted a fight, well...

I'm your huckleberry.
- Doc Holliday, Tombstone

But this is where I had it wrong. I tried to use my grit to just push forward. I tried to lock my jaw and refuse to back down. This is the exact opposite of what you should do to combat anxiety. Anxiety comes from an influx of stimulatory hormones and neurotransmitters. Through my use of mental and physical grit to resist my symptoms, the underlying biological cause was amplified even more. My production of norepinephrine and other neurotransmitters were already heightened from my mental struggles. My conscious decision to fight intensified their release even more.

Anxiety isn't just as easy as flipping off a worry switch. I've heard it described as "you have to convince yourself that the lion is not in the room." On the surface, that makes sense. But don't you think during all those times I felt like I was going to swallow my tongue that I thought, "Hey, I should try to worry less"? That occurred to me a time or two.

The problem is anxiety doesn't extend only from rational fears. My symptoms persisted even when there was absolutely nothing in the world wrong. The triggers of anxiety can be just as complex and confounding as the symptoms themselves.

Anxiety stems from a perspective problem. It comes from looking back or looking forward. Peace comes from living now. From looking at the world around me right now and being in it. Receiving from it. Adding to it.

The sparrow's not worried about tomorrow
Or the troubles to come
The lily's not thinking about the seasons
The drought or the flood
The tree that's planted by the water
Isn't fazed by the fire
So why should I be?
'Cause you take good care of me
You know what I need before I even ask a thing
And you hold me in your hands
With a kindness that never ends
I'm carried in your love, no matter what the future brings
- "Sparrows" by Cory Asbury

    I found my reprieve from anxiety in a perspective shift. I found it not by changing the what of my life but the why. I exercised before and I exercise now. The difference is I exercise now because I get to, not because I feel like I have to. The same is true with work, productivity, and all other activities in life.

    That's how you realize the lion is not in the room. Not by trying to force your brain into submission with constant thoughts like, "Everything is okay. You are fine! CALM DOWN!"

    That is the typical trajectory of despair for someone who has suffered from anxiety for an extended period of time. You start by trying to calmly implement the habits and thoughts you know are supposed to ease your symptoms. In my experience, you then see those aren't working (at least not fast enough), so you start to worry even more. Instead of the coping mechanism helping, now you just have an additional thing to worry about. *Maybe I'm not breathing just right? Maybe I'm not tilting my head just so?*

    Then frustration and fear start to take over. Anger with yourself for not being able to control your mind. Fear of the symptoms you know you are about to experience. Despair because of the feelings of ineptitude. This all culminates in a full blown attack—both by the anxiety and your own thoughts about not being able to stop the anxiety.

    The next time you feel anxiety coming on, instead of trying to convince your brain the lion isn't in the room, just slow down for a minute. Stop trying to control everything. Stop trying to make everything be just right.

    Then just open your eyes and look around. I would bet good money you're going to discover there isn't a lion in your living room. If there is, you have to admit, even though you are in pretty grave danger, that's still pretty awesome to have a lion randomly show up in your living room. So it's still a good thing you looked.

The times the lion isn't there though, you're probably going to discover what you are worrying about isn't as bad as it seemed. Driving on the interstate isn't a guaranteed death sentence. All the people in a crowded place aren't going to invade your personal space and be super weird toward you.

Even so, the best thing of all is that sometimes you are going to discover that maybe things are in fact pretty bad. Things are rough. You should be worried. But now, you are actually here in this moment where the problem really is. When you stop to look, you'll see the lion has morphed into something else. An assignment that needs to be completed. A tough conversation you need to have with your partner. A health issue you should receive treatment for. You can see the lion for what he really is. Now you can do something about it.

Anxiety Action Challenge

Meditation is the single most useful tool I've found in combating my anxiety. It's how I force myself to stop long enough to unclench my eyes and scan for the lion. Once I see him for who he is, I can follow these steps I learned from Jeff Warren, a meditation teacher. The method is called RAIN.

- Recognize - Notice your symptoms as they begin. Recognize the situations that bring them on. Feel the sensations that lead to your episodes of anxiety.
    - Another term for this is mindfulness. Be in the moment. When you live in this second, things can't sneak up on you so much. There's not so much to worry about because you can see what you're dealing with.
- Accept - Now, this will be counter-intuitive, but you have to accept your symptoms. If you try to tell yourself "don't think of ___," you're going to think of ___ over and over. Trying to run from your symptoms or ignore them doesn't work. Trying to beat them into submission like I did doesn't work either. So instead of running or fighting, just sit back and accept their presence.
    - For me, I had to accept the constant gagging feeling. I had to accept the heaviness in my chest and my inability to breathe.
- Investigate - Then, once you've accepted them, become curious about them. Investigate them. Look at them from all angles. How exactly does this symptom feel? Where does it start? Where does it move to?
    - My impulse against an object in my path is to just to try to bull through it. When I would try to tighten up and resist my symptoms, it just made them worse. I started using my knowledge of anatomy here. Instead of furiously fighting back, I just examined it all.
    - When I would tense my body, I was tightening the diaphragm so my breathing became more shallow. Anxiety was making my chest feel heavy. My tense reactions to anxiety had been assisting it in doing so.
    - When I get frustrated, I clench my teeth.

                Anxiety was causing the muscles in my throat to tighten and bringing on the gagging sensation. My tense reaction to anxiety had been assisting it in doing so.
        - Once I started understanding my symptoms, they became less scary. My heavy chest and gagging had anatomical explanations. These scary symptoms have natural causes, and once we understand the problem, we can actually begin to deal with it.
   - Non-identification - This is less of an action than an attitude. It is the attitude of not taking my emotions personally. It's seeing your emotions just as a natural toll of things. It is the acceptance that these attacks may come, but they will also go away.
        - When we open to a feeling, particularly one that comes again and again, we take the wind out of its sails. We take away the fear of the unknown.

- Instead of writing something down for this action challenge, I want you to take five minutes and practice RAIN as it is described above. Simply find a comfortable spot and:
    - Recognize how you feel in this moment.
    - Accept that it is okay to feel that way. Even if it is a negative feeling, negative feelings are just as natural as positive ones.
    - Investigate what you're feeling. Put a name to it. Bring it out into the light and really look at it.
    - Non-identification - Just be okay with it. Be okay if you feel good right now. Be okay if you don't. And accept that this moment won't last forever, whether it is good or bad. You only get so many moments in life. Live them all.

Lifestyle Change:

Take your foot off the gas. On purpose. Every day.

Value yourself when you are doing nothing. When you get nothing accomplished. Are you giving anything to the world then? I'd argue you're giving more to the world in that moment than ever before. Because you're loving yourself. And love is our purpose on Earth anyway. So slow down enough to live in the reality of your life as it is, not in how you are trying to force it to be.

This week, every day for five minutes, stop being Jan. Stop worrying about everything that needs to be done. Be Michael. Which means do nothing. Just chill. Enjoy yourself. Have fun. Laugh. Live. Give yourself permission to just be for five minutes a day.

The truth is the world will still be turning after those five minutes. Your family will still be okay. Your work will still be okay. The whole world is still okay even though you took five minutes to yourself. Life will still be okay. So you can be too.

Lesson 8: invisible illness is real (and sometimes the scars you can't see hurt the most).

We confess to God for forgiveness. We confess to each other for healing.
— Craig Groeschel, pastor and author

Mysteriously and in ways that are totally remote from normal experience, the gray drizzle of horror induced by depression takes on the quality of physical pain. But it is not an immediately identifiable pain, like that of a broken limb. It may be more accurate to say that despair, owing to some evil trick played upon the sick brain by the inhabiting psyche, comes to resemble the diabolical discomfort of being imprisoned in a fiercely overheated room. And because no breeze stirs this caldron, because there is no escape from the smothering confinement, it is entirely natural that the victim begins to think ceaselessly of oblivion.
— William Styron, Darkness Visible

Hopefully, the lessons up to this point have done an adequate job of describing what mental health problems are. Still, knowing what they are is quite different from knowing how they feel. Science hasn't developed enough to allow us to quantify how it feels to be a prisoner in the cage of your own mind.

I was that prisoner for years. The first three years of my daughter's life, the problem became worse. When I should've been rejoicing with the gift of this beautiful angel, I was fighting to just stay alive for her.

To attempt a methodical presentation of the subject is very difficult, as psychology requires a certain scientific detachment. But does a man who makes his observations while he himself is a prisoner possess the necessary detachment? Such detachment is granted to the outsiders, but he is too far removed to make any real statements of value. Only the man on the inside knows.
— Viktor E. Frankl, Man's Search For Meaning

Science cannot measure the strength of the emotion a dad feels when he kisses his little girl goodbye. It can't compute what it does to that man's heart when he tells her how much he loves her and that she's the most important thing in the whole wide world.

There's no test that assesses what it feels like for that dad to be driving down I-75 South from Midway to Richmond, pass a semi-truck, and think, "I wonder if they would think it was an accident."

We can't calculate the confusion that dad feels seconds later when he wonders how he would even consider removing himself from the world. We don't have a neat little chart of symptoms to diagnose how overwhelming it can be for him to know he considered killing himself, not because of his lack of love for that little girl, but because of the intensity of it.

We can't quantify how confusing it is for him that he wants to give that little girl the whole world but wholeheartedly believes the best way to do this is for him to no longer be in the world with her. We don't have a scale that can balance the intensity of that man's pain as he tries weighing his undying need to protect that little girl with his certainty that his insidious poison may one day infect her too.

We cannot count hormonal levels or neurotransmitter imbalances enough to justify the certainty he feels in the deepest part of his core that he deserves all of this pain.

We have no unit of measure for the hopelessness he feels knowing his brain is telling him lies but feeling powerless against believing them.

No beaker measures the shame he feels for considering suicide. No test tube estimates the dread of knowing he'll consider it again and again.

We don't have a blood test that reveals the level of contempt he feels for himself because he was willing to end it all if everyone would believe it was an accident.

He never considers a planned suicide. Never. Not once. These thoughts are never premeditated. They come in flashes. Sometimes they happen several days in a row. Then he has reprieve for weeks or months. Then one day he drives by a truck and thinks again, "I wonder if they would all think it was an accident?"

That's part of the torture. He isn't in control of it. He is Charlie Brown with Lucy pulling the football away as he goes to kick it. She leaves it there for him sometimes. Sometimes he gets to kick it. Sometimes he gets to drive to work and back home with no problems. Those are the good days.

But sometimes she pulls the ball away. It's the not knowing. The unpredictability. It is the helplessness of not being able to stop it or even knowing when he'll have to try to stop it. It is the darkness so opaque he can no longer see. The darkness that devours his entire life but is invisible to the rest of the world. It makes him feel isolated. Alone. Crazy.

He doesn't feel faith anymore. Or peace. Or joy. Or love. But he feels this. Every day he feels this. So its invisibility doesn't make it less real. It makes it more real. In fact, sometimes it's the only thing he is certain is real.

And most damning of all is the deterioration this causes on that man's mind, heart, and soul. We don't have a vaccine for the dread of living with knowing that one day the conditions—an icy road, heavy fog, pounding sleet covering his windshield—may be just right. One day everyone may think it was just an accident.

Invisible Illness Action Challenge

- Describe a pain or problem you deal with (now or in the past) that people cannot see.

I remember your bare feet down the hallway
I remember your little laugh
Race cars on the kitchen floor, plastic dinosaurs
I love you to the moon and back
I remember your blue eyes looking into mine
Like we had our own secret club
I remember you dancing before bed time
Then jumping on me, waking me up
I can still feel you hold my hand, little man
And even the moment I knew
You fought it hard like an army guy
Remember I leaned in and whispered to you
Come on baby with me, we're gonna fly away from here
You were my best four years
I remember the drive home
When the blind hope turned to crying and screaming "Why?"
Flowers pile up in the worst way, no one knows what to say
About a beautiful boy who died
And it's about to be Halloween
You could be anything you wanted if you were still here

> *I remember the last day when I kissed your face*
> *And whispered in your ear*
> *Come on baby with me, we're gonna fly away from here*
> *Out of this curtained room in this hospital grey,*
> *we'll just disappear*
> *Come on baby with me, we're gonna fly away from here*
> *You were my best four years*
> *What if I'm standing in your closet trying to talk to you?*
> *What if I kept the hand-me-downs you won't grow into?*
> *And what if I really thought some miracle would see us through?*
> *What if the miracle was even getting one moment with you?*
> *Come on baby with me, we're gonna fly away from here*
> *Come on baby with me, we're gonna fly away from here*
> *You were my best four years*
> *I remember your bare feet down the hallway*
> *I love you to the moon and back*
> - "Ronan" by Taylor Swift

I included these lyrics because Taylor Swift is Georgia's favorite singer. She wrote this song by pulling lines from the blog of a mother who's four-year-old son was dying from cancer. That baby died. That mother had to keep going. She had to endure pain I cannot imagine. I don't think I've ever listened to that song without crying. I don't know her, and I cannot fathom the strength it would take to carry on after such a loss.

I would never try to compare my pain to hers—or anyone else's—but she and I have singular blast points from which mental health issues could typically arise. We have specific instances people on the outside can point to and say, "That's what caused their depression." That helps people feel more comfortable with invisible illness. It makes the invisible more visible. More tangible.

But depression is so much more than a reaction to a singular moment. We've already talked about the unrealistic expectations we place on ourselves and how mental health issues can begin well before anyone else can see them. Maybe you've never lost anyone. Maybe you have the perfect life. At least, everybody tells you that you do. Maybe you have everything anyone could ever want. At least, everybody tells you that you do. Maybe you don't even know why you feel the way you feel.

That doesn't mean your struggles are any less real than mine or the mother who lost her four-year-old son to cancer. You don't have to meet anyone else's standards of external pain to be able to reach out for help. Just because your pain is invisible to the world doesn't mean it is less real.

You wouldn't think you were weird or flawed if you had really black hair or really blonde hair. Those things aren't embarrassing to have. Black hair is just the heavy production of the protein melanin while blonde hair comes from a lighter production.

Well, mental health is mainly determined by the production of neurotransmitters that pass messages between neurons (nerve cells) in the brain and body. Many of these neurotransmitters are proteins as well. They determine when you feel happy, sad, angry, etc. The overproduction or underproduction of one of these neurotransmitters creates real issues. The only difference is you can see your hair but you cannot see your mental health.

- Look back at the problem you described at the start of this action challenge. How have you been brave enough to share your struggles with others even though they can't see them? Explain.

Lifestyle change:
If someone says to you that they have depression, don't ask why. There is no why...
I'm not a professional depressed person. I am so much more than that. I am very lucky. I do have amazing, beautiful things in my life. I am so very full of love...
That's the thing about potential; it was so close, what could have been but didn't happen and will never happen. The events did not line up perfectly. And it breaks your heart.
- Elisa Lam, Crime Scene: The Vanishing at Cecil Hotel

Sarah is a true-crime junkie. As such, we've listened to a couple podcasts and watched the Netflix documentary about the death of Elisa Lam. She was found in a water tower on the roof of the Cecil Hotel after having been missing for nineteen days. It's one of the most conspiracy-theory riddled cases in American history. Theories range from supernatural influences to murder to police cover-up.

The truth is Elisa was a 21-year-old girl with severe mental health issues. She wasn't taking her medication and had a lapse from reality. She died because of a tragic accident as a result of her bipolar disorder, but it's much more glorious to conjure up ghosts and alternate dimensions. Or much spookier to imagine a vicious murderer. The truth is much simpler. The truth is much sadder. The truth is Elisa lost a battle to an invisible enemy many people are fighting today.

Since other people can't see your pain, you can choose to ignore your issues. I know. I did. Or tried to at least. It's easy to accept less out of life than you deserve. Elisa Lam did. She stopped taking her medication. In her social media posts, she lamented about being dependent on so many daily meds. She couldn't see her problems, so they felt less real.

She wanted to be "normal." She felt like if she did enough "normal things" on the outside, then she'd think and feel normal on the inside. She wanted to be adventurous. She went on a vacation to Los Angeles by herself. She thought that if she was strong enough to do this by herself, she was strong enough to beat her mental health issues by herself. If she did enough fun things in enough fun places, then all the invisible pain would go away. It didn't. And she lost her life because of it.

It's hard to see justice sometimes. It's hard to see fairness despite the events in your life that may not have lined up perfectly. Maybe you've gotten the raw end of the deal more than your share of times. But you're still here. Whatever has happened, your fight isn't over. You still have a chance. The only question now is what you will do with it. Because to waste this opportunity at life while so many others have lost it, that would be the greatest injustice of all.

Today, make the invisible visible. Speak out about your troubles. You don't have to battle alone, suffering in silence. No, you can't see your pain. You can't see love either. Or peace. Or joy. Or faith. Or many of the most real things in the world.

Love others by letting them love you. That's what the true people in your life want to do. They want to help and be there for you. But first, you have to be willing to let them.

And for those of you who aren't in that dark place, please know this. In all the lessons of this series, not a single time did the person realize they were teaching me. Not one. They just loved. And they lived. They lived a loving life. Lives that cut through the darkness for me. Lives that saved mine. No one knew I was the life that needed to be saved, but they lived their life in a way that made me want to hang on to mine a little bit longer.

So don't go try to teach the world. People don't learn lessons when you're trying to teach them. Just go live a loving life. Go live a life that cuts through the darkness for someone. Not just the people screaming out for help. But for people like me, people who had given up on screaming. Go live a life that saves someone else's.

Some people have fallen, and they're no longer reaching up for help. If no one comes along to interfere, they're just going to stay on the floor until their life ends either by natural causes or them taking it themselves. You never know which smiling face is planning to make this day their last.

So reach love down to your kids and students. Reach love over to your friends and siblings. Reach love up to your parents and role-models. Reach love out for the lives that may be on the verge of being lost. Reach love out for the life you'll save and the lives they'll save in return.

Part 2: Meet my wife, Sarah Reid, who taught me...

Our wedding day: 10-19-20
Check out our four-minute wedding video on the Love is Real Wellness YouTube Channel. I don't have the link to share (because the video released the same day as this book), but the title of the video is "Love Redeems Release Special - Our Wedding Video_ARM Ep 174" My unbiased opinion: it's awesome.

George in Sarah's words:
- I never had the pleasure of physically meeting George, but I have heard countless stories and memories that give me insight into the kind of person that he was. Bravery, sense of humor, and incredible artistic talent are just some of the qualities I can use to describe him.
- George has helped shape Adam into the amazing person he is today. I would say George was a blessing to those who were fortunate enough to have him touch their lives in some way, and I am grateful to him for the impact he has had on Adams' life.

Lifestyle change:
Throughout this series, the definition of love used is to show someone their beauty, worth, and importance. Love is the most powerful force on Earth. It is the light to vanquish the darkness of the world. But this can only happen if love is real. In every day and in every way, allow love to be real in your life. You do this by loving for the sake of loving—never expecting recognition, praise, or reciprocation. Love yourself freely. Love your neighbor fully. Love because you deserve it. Love because they deserve it. Love because we all deserve it.

<u>Lesson 9: intimacy is real (and it isn't as scary as it seems).</u>
I know a lot of guys say they're thankful they found wives that make them want to be a better man.
I didn't find that. You don't make me want to be a better man.
I've wanted that my whole life and never felt like I was enough.
I have worked with everything I have in everything I have ever done, until I met you.
With you, I've never had to try. From our beginning to our end, we just are. We were meant to be.
You don't make me want to be better. You make me want to be me. You make me want to actually live life.
You are the life I never prayed for because I never thought I deserved.
You are the best, most pure person I have ever known. You give so freely that you don't even know you've given.
The world is a better place because you're in it. You are the woman I want Georgia to grow up to be.
So, I won't try to be better for you.
I'll do the thing I was never able to do until I met you. I'll do the scariest, hardest thing in the world.
I'll just be me.
You've given me the gift of knowing that is enough. And I will love you with everything in me for the rest of my life.
- *My wedding vows to Sarah on 10-19-20 in Yosemite National Park (Glacier Point)*

Always remember, there was nothing worth sharing
Like the love that let us share our name
- *"Murder in the City" by The Avett Brothers*

So I'll love ya till my lungs give out
I ain't lyin'
I'm all your'n and you're all mine
There ain't two ways around it
There ain't no tryin' bout it
I'm all your'n and you're all mine
- *"All Your'n" by Tyler Childers*

You are my sunshine, my only sunshine.
You make me happy when skies are gray.
You'll never know dear, how much I love you.
- *"You are My Sunshine" by Jimmie Davis and Charles Mitchell*

I cannot tell you how glad I am that I met Sarah when I did. Something tells me she wouldn't have been very interested in me during my twenties. I mean, maybe she would have been attracted to a guy who was belligerently drunk six or seven days a week. There's a chance she may have enjoyed waking up in a bed soaked in urine some nights. But, then again, she may not have.

Luckily, Sarah and I met a few months into my sobriety. Our relationship has known nothing but love. Any mistakes I've made during our time together have been made by me, not the incoherent and destructive zombie I was while blackout drunk.

I'm glad Sarah came into my life after alcohol was no longer a part of it, but that meant she met me at my absolute lowest point. I hadn't simply chosen to walk away from drinking. I had hit rock bottom with a DUI arrest four months prior that slammed the reality of my problems in my face. I had remained sober since, but it was through sheer willpower. I struggled daily with shame more than I had in my entire life (and that's saying something). I had lost all hope.

Then my sister-in-law, Mary Beth, played matchmaker with Sarah and me (Mary Beth threatened me over not getting a shout out in the first book. I feel like getting beaten up by a girl would hurt my street cred, so here's your shout out.)

From the first moment I met Sarah, I knew she was special. Not in a butterflies in my stomach way (which is an emotion called limerence that is often confused for love), but rather in admiration of who she was. Sarah is the most generous person I have ever met. She loves with every ounce of her without ever expecting anything in return.

Love means to show someone their beauty, worth, and importance. She is the epitome of this definition of love. Everything she is and everything she does shows others the beauty of themselves. She naturally is who I've always tried so hard to be.

I knew immediately she was everything I had ever wanted, so I had to pull out the big guns to impress her. Something you have to understand about me is that I'm a natural romancer. Sarah never really had a chance.

For our first date, I took her to iHop because that's what romantic people do. Then, I ordered two separate meals. Studies show that ladies love a man who can eat an inordinate amount of iHop. I don't remember much of the actual conversation from the date, but I'm sure it was mostly her swooning and trying not to pass out from excitement.

Some guys may be intuitive enough to treat their lady to the fine dining of iHop on their first date. There may even be a few chosen gentlemen who are in touch with the opposite sex enough to impress her by ordering two meals. But I'm just a cut above the rest.

I saved my smoothest move for last. When the ticket came charging three meals for two people, I reached into my pocket for my wallet—a wallet I had left on the dresser at my house.

After I let her pay for my two meals, she was understandably hooked. No other man had taken her to iHop and let her buy him two dinners at once. She realized she had landed a true Casanova. (Side note: I also forgot my wallet during one of the three most expensive dinners we've ever had. She's starting to suspect "forgetting my wallet" is strategic.)

But seriously, even after my obvious repeated gaffes, I was never embarrassed. Not even on a first date with this amazing woman who I had just met. With her, for the first time in my life, I felt okay just being me. I love iHop. I eat a lot. And I'm the most forgetful person on the planet. I wasn't afraid to show her the real me. From that moment to this one, I have never had to be more than I am.

I had never been intimate with a single person in my life. Not one. I couldn't be. I'm not talking about romantic intimacy. I'm referring to a real connection with someone else where they are allowed into every corner of your life. Even the dark, dusty ones we keep off limits, oftentimes even to ourselves. To be intimate requires being real. Being real requires showing weakness. And weakness was not something I tolerated.

I kept a wall around my life with windows open where anyone in the world could look in all they wanted. But their view through those tiny slots was limited to what I wanted them to see.

My kindness was placed directly in the center of the window's opening. My grit and determination were in plain sight. All my accomplishments—shiny teaching awards, letters from kids telling how I'd changed their lives—decorated the limited-access display.

Lots of people knew about me, but no one knew me. Not entirely. They saw through the windows but were never granted access inside the wall.

Sarah is the first person who ever actually knew me in my adult life. Or at least all of me.

Everything I had done, I had done alone. Not physically. I was surrounded by a loving family. I am a part of the tightest group of friends I know with most of us having been best friends since grade school. I had people I knew would do absolutely anything for me at any moment.

But that didn't matter because I would never call on them to do so. I was alone in the worst way. I was alone in my heart and in my mind.

I had taken pride in that. I was strong enough to never need help. But in reality, I was too weak to ask for it. I helped everyone else in every way possible, but I never accepted help in return. I spent my life dedicated to others and sacrificed myself in every way I could. Ultimately though, that was just me showing how great I am and that they needed me. To show true love, I had to let others give me love too.

I used to think I was protecting people by not unloading my problems on them. I thought I was helping them by never introducing any sense of additional burden into their life. Even so, that was me loving myself, not them. I wasn't showing them their beauty, worth, and importance. I was showing them mine.

I didn't just show Sarah the good. I showed her the bad too. Instead of me trying to be strong for both of us, we have always been strong together. More often than not, it's actually been her helping me along (once I started opening up about my need for help, it turns out I need it quite often).

I've realized allowing her to help me doesn't place a burden on her. It allows her to feel the pleasure of helping someone in need and adding value to the world. I always loved helping people because I cared about them. By opening up to her, I allow her the opportunity to achieve that same sense of gratitude that comes with fulfilling God's purpose—to love your neighbor as yourself. During my moments of weakness and need for her, I am able to show her that she matters, that she is worthy, and that she is beautiful. The most beautiful person I've ever met in fact.

Intimacy Action Challenge

Intimacy requires a real connection. It isn't based on a slide show where we highlight our greatest attributes. It is based on a reel of film that continues to roll during our meltdowns and lowest moments. It requires showing the behind the scenes bloopers we want to hide.

Before anyone else can know you, you have to know yourself. I am convinced that the majority of people have lost all real intimacy. We become so fixated on who we want to be/try to be that we lose contact with who we really are. This affects every relationship you have: with yourself, with others, and with God.

- Reconnect with yourself. List five characteristics about yourself you are proud of and five attributes you are unhappy with/wish were different.

Positive:
1)
2)
3)
4)
5)

Negative:
1)
2)
3)
4)
5)

The difference between knowledge and intimacy is knowing about Jesus and knowing Jesus.
- Kyle Idleman, Not a Fan

The same is true with ourselves. Above, you wrote a list of your traits that you interpret as positive and negative. Still, simply listing them is a surface level description. People may know those things about you. Do they know beyond those facts to how they make you feel as a person? Do they know about you, or do they actually know you?

- Using the same list as above, expand on those characteristics. When they have impacted your life?

How do they change how you feel about yourself as a person?

Positive:
1)

2)

3)

4)

5)

Negative:
1)

2)

3)

4)

5)

Lifestyle change:

If you are by yourself for more than a day, you start producing a greater number of stress hormones, your mood and energy plummet, and several key biological processes are disrupted. Being alone for extended periods of time is considered torment in most countries. Even in prison, the worst form of punishment is being isolated in the hole.

Yet, we put ourselves in the hole. We are surrounded by people and have more access to others than at any point in human history. Still, in reality, we are alone because we hide our true selves.

Intimacy isn't as scary as we make it. It's okay to show people your faults because they have faults too. Pretending we are perfect creates division because ultimately we all know we aren't these molds of the perfect person we pretend to be.

Don't presume that by showing a weakness people will see you as weak. Sometimes having a weakness and showing the strength to be able to deal with the issue makes you seem stronger than ever. Don't convince yourself that people are going to judge you for who you are.

Maybe the person you love the most doesn't need you to be strong. Maybe they need you to be weak. Maybe they need you to be weak so they can admit that sometimes they feel weak too.

Today, allow someone to read your list from above. Restore connection with yourself. Allow for a deeper relationship with those you love by sharing your true self.

Lesson 10: vulnerability is real (and telling your story with your whole heart).

I would rather bleed out than sit here and talk about my feelings for ten minutes.
- Ron Swanson, Parks and Recreation

But you keep standing at a distance
In the shadow of your shame
There's a light of hope that's shining
Won't you come and take your place?
And bring it all to the table
There's nothing He ain't seen before
For all your sin, all your sorrow, and your sadness
There's a Savior and He calls
Bring it all to the table
He can see the weight you carry
The fears that hold your heart
But through the cross you've been forgiven
You're accepted as you are
- "To the Table" by Zach Williams

[19] Again, truly I tell you that if two of you on earth agree about anything they ask for, it will be done for them by my Father in heaven. [20] For where two or three gather in my name, there I am with them.
- Matthew 18:19-20

    Even though I had my DUI on July 27th, 2018, I didn't lose my license until December 11th, 2018. The judge agreed to push back my sentencing until my school's Christmas break to limit the professional impact on me.

    Sarah and I started dating on November 4th, 2018. She lived in my hometown which was about an hour and a half from me. Less than forty days into our relationship, I lost my license for a month.

    When Christmas came, I faced my first trial for accepting vulnerability in our relationship. Sarah loves to travel. She would much rather spend money toward experiencing the world than owning possessions. I knew she would rather live life with me on some exciting trip than have a present wrapped under the tree.

    I wanted to avoid discussion of my DUI and its fallout as much as possible. If I could just stay in a hole for that month, we could move on like it never happened. I could continue to appear strong and desirable to my new girlfriend. I wanted her to see the image I had faked for everyone else my whole life.

At this point, I hadn't drank for four months, but I hadn't solved the problem in my heart. I had cleared the cobwebs in my life like I had always done, but I had left the spider.

I still had deep-rooted shame and regret. I still hated and intentionally punished myself often. Drowning in alcohol had been only one of my methods of penance. Other punishments remained behind closed doors. I have always been extremely health conscious—both through exercise and nutrition—because of George. I knew my health was a gift, and I tried to live in respect of that gift. So when I was having a downswing in my mental health, I would eat junk food late at night knowing it would make me feel terrible. And I welcomed the feeling because I thought I deserved it.

I would work through the night preparing lessons for my classroom, often sleeping only a couple hours. I would wake up with a headache. A headache that I embraced.

Vulnerability was my biggest enemy. It went against everything I believed in. It went against strength, hard work, and grit. My sheer refusal to surrender was the one way I had been able to honor George. Over the previous thirteen years, I had refused weakness. I had refused to give up or be beaten.

In my persistence, I confused never being weak with never being vulnerable. I numbed vulnerability to hold on to this illusion of strength I had created. But I wanted to make Sarah happy more than I wanted to appear strong. Acting like the man she deserved wouldn't allow me to add to her life; I had to actually be that man.

But I couldn't drive anywhere. It was pretty humiliating to say, "You get to drive two hours from Clay County to Midway to pick me up, then drive four and a half more hours to the Biltmore Estate. Merry Christmas!"

But I said it. I chose her over my pride. I told her I wanted to live life with her, but I needed her help. I told her I had made lots of mistakes, but she made me want to leave those mistakes behind.

So we went. She drove the six-and-a-half hours it took to do so. Although I didn't know it as we headed off on our trip, I was on more roads than one. We were going down I-75 South to Asheville, North Carolina, but I was also finally starting down the road to real recovery. And Sarah was beside me for both.

Vulnerability is a four-letter word to most people. It definitely was to me. But only when you embrace vulnerability is true human connection possible.

No one loves the idea of being vulnerable. It isn't exciting to embrace the possibility of failure and rejection, but you must accept vulnerability as a natural component of a healthy life.

Intimacy requires vulnerability. It requires the risk of allowing someone to see you in your raw nakedness. You have to let someone see your scars and simply hope they will see them as part of your strength and beauty. You pray they see past your blemishes to the story they tell. Vulnerability requires giving up control and giving other people the freedom to have their own interpretations and conclusions.

Vulnerability isn't only vital to your relationship with others. It's essential to your relationship with yourself. Authenticity requires vulnerability. To be real, you have to be willing to accept both the successes and failures of your life. You have to be able to accept that failure is an option to give yourself an opportunity to succeed.

Someone who claims to never have problems and never need help isn't strong. They are weak. I know. I've been there. Living that life doesn't make you strong. It makes you fake. Vulnerability is the only way to overcome shame. Vulnerability is the only way to rid ourselves of the secrecy, the silence, and the judgment.

In *Love is Real*, I referenced Brené Brown's Ted Talk "The Power of Vulnerability." She spent six years studying shame to find what connection existed between people who she referred to as "whole-hearted." The unifying characteristic of whole-hearted people was they proclaimed to have authentic love, peace, and joy in their lives. Her years of research unearthed a conclusion that originally seemed like a waste of a whole lot of money, effort, and time to me: Whole-hearted people simply believed they were worthy of love and belonging. The one thing allowing these people to experience true connection with others is that they believe they are worthy of connection.

If it's as simple as believing we're worthy, then it seems like we should just believe we are worthy. Flip on that switch and feel better. Yet millions of people are not whole-hearted. Millions of people do not have peace. They do not have joy. They do not have love. What allows some people to accept their self-worth while others struggle to find it?

Brené Brown found four commonalities that allowed these individuals to accept their importance and beauty regardless of their success or failure.

1. Courage - Courage comes from the Latin word "cor," which means heart. The original definition of courage was to tell the story of who you are with your whole heart. Whole-hearted people had the

courage to be imperfect. They had the courage to tell their story as it really was, not as they wished it had been.
2. Compassion - Research shows you can't be truly compassionate toward others if you can't show compassion to yourself. Without kindness to yourself, whatever tenderness you show other people is an imitation of what you think compassion is.
3. Connection - Whole-hearted people had strong bonds to others as a result of authenticity. They formed real relationships because they let go of who they thought they should be in order to be who they were.
4. Vulnerability - They believed that what made them vulnerable made them beautiful. Vulnerability wasn't comfortable for them, but they didn't describe it as excruciating either. They simply accepted it was necessary. They were willing to say "I love you" first. They pursued their desires without guarantees.

In the deepest sense, I am a scientist. These findings show with undeniable amounts of data that vulnerability is necessary to avoid shame, fear, and feelings of unworthiness. Not only that, but vulnerability is also the birthplace of joy, creativity, belonging, and love.

Professor Brown called these people whole-hearted because their willingness to experience the lows actually gave them the capacity to experience the highs. When you accept that you are just as worthy of love when you fail as when you succeed, then the gravity of rejection is not so strong. You can experience failure as what it is—a natural part of life—rather than proof of your worthlessness.

I started admitting when I am weak and when I need help. I exposed the reason I slept with the television on was because I couldn't be alone with my thoughts. I confessed that the reason I am good is because I am terrified to be bad. I conceded that I work so hard because I have to give to the world to feel like I have any value.

I got rid of the secrecy and the silence. I chose to live a life of truth and freedom in pursuit of peace rather than a life of fake strength chained by the expectations I put on myself. Whatever struggles I face for the rest of my life, I won't let shame cause me to suffer in silence. I'll face those struggles in truth. At last, I'll face those struggles in strength.

Vulnerability Action Challenge

In some ways, failure feels like a dirty little secret because people rarely want to discuss their own failures. But in reality, we're all wearing masks to cover our shortcomings, all thinking that the feelings of self-doubt and misgiving are ours alone. Nothing could be further from the truth; failure is part of being human.
- Tony Dungy, Uncommon

How ironic, I thought. Here I am, a spokesman for the All Pro Dad program, helping others to be better parents, and my child took his own life. I figure this would wipe out any credibility I might have had.
- Tony Dungy, Quiet Strength

    I have loved football my whole life. I grew up playing it and spent years coaching. Tony Dungy is one of my role-models in the sport. He was the first African American head coach to win a Super Bowl. More importantly, he is a man of integrity, honor, and Christian faith. In these two passages, he encompasses the complexities of vulnerability.
    Nothing is more important to me than my role as Georgia's Daddy. Nothing. Everything I am and everything I do is impacted by my responsibility as her father. As I struggled with shame during Georgia's first couple years, my love for her allowed the roots of regret to penetrate my heart even deeper. Georgia deserved more than me. She deserved someone better.
    Tony Dungy's son committed suicide when he was eighteen years old. I cannot imagine the turmoil and guilt Tony must've felt as he replayed his son's eighteen years over and over again in his mind. Where did things go wrong? How could I have prevented this? How could I have failed my son so much that he was blinded to my love for him?
    I can't put myself in that place. I cannot do it. I just don't know if I would be strong enough to keep on living if Georgia took her own life. But Tony was brave enough to stand up in front of a group that was built around being good dads. He told them about how his son died. He told them of all of the good times they shared. He told them of his regret and of the dangers of mental health struggles. He was courageous enough

to tell his story with his whole heart.

Someone in that audience needed to hear Tony's story. They didn't need to shake the hand of a Super Bowl winning head coach. They didn't need to take a picture with a future Hall of Famer. This person didn't need to hear about his success. They needed to hear about his failure. Someone needed to hear that loving parents can still lose their children. Someone needed to know that mental health problems are a disease, and they are not the fault of the parent nor the person suffering from them. Someone needed to know that they were not alone in the world.

- Describe a painful failure in your life you have intentionally hidden from others. Maybe you've shared this with a few, select people you trust. Maybe, like me, you haven't shared it with anyone. Tell what happened and how it impacted you.

- Do you think anyone else has ever experienced something like what you described above? How could sharing your story help them heal?

Lifestyle change:
For thirteen years, I hid my pain. I hid my depression, anxiety, alcoholism, despair, shame, regret, and so much more. I'm not hiding anymore. If you or anyone you know was helped by *Love is Real*, then you have experienced firsthand how one person accepting vulnerability can help someone else.

Believe me when I say I know how difficult this is. It is so difficult to step out on that ledge of vulnerability and allow someone to actually know you. If they actually know you, then they can hurt you. It's hard to give someone that power over your life.

Give of yourself not for you. Give of yourself for everyone else. Be vulnerable so the people you love can be vulnerable too. Talk to someone today. Share your story with your whole heart. You are a gift to the world. Share yourself completely. Someone out there needs you to.

<u>Lesson 11: numbing emotions is real (and you cannot selectively numb the bad ones).</u>

The quickest way to reach the sun and the light of day is not to turn west chasing after it, but to head east into the darkness until you reach the sunrise.
- Gerald Lawson Sittser, A Grace Disguised

Only forgiveness and the determination to live rightly before God can bring a clear conscience. How important Job's record became as he was being accused. Like Job, we can't claim sinless lives, but we can claim forgiven lives. When we confess our sins to God, He forgives us. Then, we can live with clear consciences.
- Life Application Study Bible, Job 27:6 description

Catastrophic loss by definition precludes recovery. It will transform us or destroy us, but it will never leave us the same. There is no going back to the past, which is gone forever, only going ahead to the future, which has yet to be discovered.
- Peter Scazzero, Emotionally Healthy Spirituality

Society teaches us that having feelings and crying is bad and wrong. Well, that's baloney because grief isn't wrong. There's such a thing as good grief. Just ask Charlie Brown.
- Michael Scott, The Office

A few months later, I realized I was in love with Sarah Milligan Burchell.

She came up to visit me on Saturday, and we were supposed to go out on a fancy date. As you have already read, I am the definition of romance. Spontaneity is key to a relationship. As such, I didn't take her out to the nice date she had been looking forward to. I switched it up for something better. I let her do hard, manual labor all day long in the blazing heat of summer.

Our church hosts a local community service event called "Mission Midway" every year. I had forgotten all about it until Sarah got to my house, so I sprung the great news on her. "You know that tasty dinner we were going to? You don't have to bother yourself with getting ready for that. Your casual clothes are just fine for what we've got in store today."

Sarah and I were working with a group that was pulling weeds from the local park. We worked from 9 AM to 2 PM essentially nonstop. I know that doesn't sound like a lot, but five hours on your hands and knees pulling weeds is pretty tough.

When it came time to stop for the day, I looked around but couldn't find her. Everyone was near the parking lot, but she wasn't with them. I walked back through the park to find her. When I saw her, she still had her bucket and was pulling weeds.

All the other volunteers were finished. All the church members who were supposed to be the official participants in Mission Midway were done. The self-proclaimed toughest man pound-for-pound and hardest worker alive (me) was done. She wasn't. She knew everyone else was done, but she wasn't.

Being in a relationship doesn't create intimacy. Vulnerability does. Being willing to let someone truly see you. When I saw Sarah squatting down pulling weeds, I really saw her. I saw past what she was doing—dirty, sweaty work—to who she was. That's when I knew she was the person I want Georgia to grow up to be: A woman who realizes the world is bigger than her. Someone who is willing to give all of herself.

After I looked at Sarah and saw her—truly saw her—I decided to let her see me.

That should be it, right? Man struggles for a long time. Meets a woman who helps him decide to share those struggles. Together they overcome.

But it wasn't quite so simple. Turns out there's a reason people avoid negative emotions. Turns out bad stuff doesn't feel good. In fact, it feels bad.

At first, when I opened my Pandora's box of emotions, things didn't get better. They got worse. The gagging. The smothering. This is when it really amplified. Just when I decided I wanted to get better, the symptoms I had been fighting in secrecy got severely worse.

You cannot selectively numb emotion. You can't say here's the bad stuff: vulnerability, shame, grief, disappointment. I don't want to feel these. You cannot just numb these. When you numb these, you desensitize yourself to all emotion. We numb joy, gratitude, all positive emotions.
- Brené Brown

I didn't understand during thirteen years of denying and avoiding my shame that shutting off the pain, bitterness, and anger numbed all my emotions. I was avoiding the heartache I had buried deep down, but I was also losing any chance at love or joy. With Sarah, I wanted to open my heart to joy, but I was also opening it to pain and strife. I had shut myself off to any negative emotion for so long that they all came rushing back in like a tidal wave when I opened myself back up.

    This naturally made me want to stop talking. Stop sharing. Go back into my hole. Just suck it up and keep going. I was faced with a decision: feel everything or feel nothing. I chose everything.

Numbing Emotions Action Challenge
- How do you react, both internally and externally, when you experience each of the following emotions:
  - Anger:

  - Sadness:

  - Regret:

  - Disappointment:

  - Shame:

I would rather Georgia have her heart broken a hundred times than live life too afraid to love. Trust me, I never want her to feel pain. Most of my life is spent ensuring that doesn't happen. But if it comes down to feeling pain or feeling nothing at all, the choice is easy for me.

You can't live your life preventing any possible harm from ever coming your way. A life without risk is no life at all. You also can't ignore feelings of anger, sadness, etc. God designed you to feel. You're not the only person in the world to have these feelings; it just feels that way because we're all too afraid to admit them. Address them in a healthy way. Accept the negative in your life. Accept the nature of being human. Only then can you truly experience the good.
- Look back at the descriptions above of how you respond to negative emotions. How could you react in a healthier way to each of these?
  - Anger:

  - Sadness:

- Regret:

- Disappointment:

- Shame:

Lifestyle change:
Let yourself be seen. Love with your whole heart even though there is no guarantee you'll be loved back. Love your friends even though they may turn their backs on you during tough times. Love the stranger on the street even though you have no reason to believe they deserve it. Love everyone because everyone deserves to be loved, even those who will let you down.

Love knowing it will bring some of the most painful experiences of your life. But, accepting this truth, learn to truly appreciate the times when someone does love you back. Learn to cherish the people who don't leave when times get tough. To feel this vulnerable is to be alive.

Today, open yourself to whatever negative circumstance or emotion you have been avoiding. You choose how you do so. Journal. Call a friend. Meditate.

The longer you run from this issue, the larger the shadow it casts over your life. Walk directly up to the problem and look it in the face. More than likely, you'll discover the monster in the closet was just a coat. But for some of you, the monstrous problem you've been running from will be real. Well, it's still a pretty good thing you looked. Living with a monster constantly lurking in the shadows isn't a very comfortable life. Deal with the reality of your situation, and usher the monster out of your house.

Lesson 12: ignorance is real (and it's your fault if you choose to stay ignorant).

The Bible wasn't written for those who have it figured out, but instead it is God's Word to those of us who are muddling through life. We must remember that "all have sinned and fall short of the glory of God," but we have been given the freedom through Christ to forget the past and look forward to what lies ahead as we "press on to reach the end of the race."
- Tony Dungy, Uncommon

[24.] *Do you not know that in a race all the runners run, but only one gets the prize? Run in such a way as to get the prize.* [25.] *Everyone who competes in the games goes into strict training. They do it to get a crown that will not last, but we do it to get a crown that will last forever.* [26.] *Therefore I do not run like someone running aimlessly; I do not fight like a boxer beating the air.* [27.] *No, I strike a blow to my body and make it my slave so that after I have preached to others, I myself will not be disqualified for the prize.*
- 1 Corinthians 9:24-27 (MCHS FCA motto)

I searched the world but it couldn't fill me
Man's empty praise and treasures that fade
Are never enough
Then You came along and put me back together
And every desire is now satisfied
Here in Your love
...
I'm not afraid to show You my weakness
My failures and flaws, Lord, You've seen 'em all
And You still call me friend
'Cause the God of the mountain is the God of the valley
There's not a place Your mercy and grace
Won't find me again
Oh, there's nothing better than You
- "Graves and Gardens" by Elevation Worship

I did not know that I was supposed to feel everything. I thought I was supposed to feel happy.
- Glennon Doyle

If we don't change our direction, we are likely to end up where we are headed.
- Ancient Chinese Proverb

I had spent my life consumed by achievement. Every waking moment was spent working toward a goal. My greatest pride was my work ethic. The influence of my uncle George and Dad had inspired me to be tenacious in my pursuit of perfection. It originated from wanting to honor these two great men, but it had degraded to a lifestyle of avoidance. I constantly had to *do* so I would never have to *be*. I had to achieve so that I wouldn't be a failure. After all, the antonyms of achievement are defeat, loss, and forfeit. These things went beyond unacceptable in my eyes. They disgusted me.

After I met Sarah, the goals I had spent my life grinding toward no longer seemed to matter so much. I took my eyes off the prize for a second and realized everything to the left and to the right of my narrow road to success was barren wasteland. I had focused so intensely on the things I was working toward in my life that I had left everything else to crumble away. The rubble contained the things that really matter: peace, joy, faith, and love.

> *It's not just picture perfect dancing in a white dress*
> *It's not just rainy days where nothing stops the fighting*
> *It's not just highs and lows and champagne toasts*
> *I've come to know that love's not only*
> *The best days or the worst days*
> *Love is the Tuesdays*
> *- "Tuesdays" by Jake Scott (our wedding dance song)*

Sarah finally opened my eyes to reality. She didn't make the big moments matter. She made every moment matter. That's where life happens: in the seemingly small, inconsequential times. Not during your most reprehensible failure or during your crowning achievement, but during the preparation for both of those events. Who you are on a second-by-second basis determines who you'll be when that test or triumph comes. She gave me a reason to want to feel. She gave me a reason to want to truly live.

A lot of people suffering have been doing so for so long they no longer realize they are in pain. We forget what it even feels like to not suffer. We accept struggling to survive each day as normal. When George first died, I was well aware of my mental health struggles but refused to reach out for help. It was a self-enforced penance. I deserved to feel pain, so I welcomed it. But thirteen years later, George's death was no longer the epicenter of the storm in my life. Ignorance was.

The root word of ignorance is "ignore." Ignorance is born through willfully ignoring the facts or allowing yourself to remain unaware of them. Depression builds and builds because at first we don't realize what's happening. Everybody has days when we feel pain and heartache. It's natural, especially after loss. In fact, it is healthy to mourn and ruminate for a period following traumatic events.

The problem is that there is no definitive time period when you can expect to feel better. "I'm struggling today, but tomorrow I'm sure I'll feel a little better."

If you stick your hand into a steaming hot bath, you would pull away quickly. On the other hand, if you acclimate yourself to a warm bath, you can continue to funnel in increasingly hotter water. Eventually, you are tolerating a temperature even higher than what signaled extreme pain when you just stuck your hand in.

The same is true with other mental health issues. They sneak up on you. Through your acclimation to the constant sense of despair and hopelessness, depression can gradually erode your mental and physical well-being without you ever realizing what's happening.

Everyone knows the word depression, so they think they get what it's all about. Most people have no idea. Because they never experience it, it can't be described in a feasible manner.

It's the same thing with my colorblindness. Inevitably, after asking me what color their shirt is, people will always ask, "What does the world look like to you?" I try to explain out of politeness even though I know it is a futile exercise. I don't see what you see, and you don't see what I see. It is impossible to make a comparison because the "colors" in my world do not exist in yours and vice versa. I lack the functioning color photoreceptors (cones) to pick up certain wavelengths of light. You have learned to identify "red" simply through repetition. As a kid, you were shown a red object and asked what color it was. After lots of trials, you began to associate all things of that color with the name "red." You can do that because every time they show you a red object, it looks red (and anything they show you that is a different color does not appear red).

For me, no matter how many different "red" objects are put in front of me, I don't begin to categorize them as "red" because I cannot see the pattern of similar colors. Instead of having cones to pick up all the different wavelengths of light, I am only able to pick up a few of them; therefore, all the different variations of color that appear similar to you are all the exact same to me. Show me something red. Then show me something pink. Lastly, have me look at something purple. To you, you've shown me three colors. To me, you've shown me one.

The clearest explanation I've been able to give is to tell people to open the "Paint" program on a computer. There will be lots of different color options to choose from. You may see twenty or so different blocks of color. I will see four or five. There is no difference in purple, maroon, red, etc. I see merely one color that is some intermediate of all of these colors. So, although people refuse to give up and end up asking me what color ten different things in our vicinity are, I simply cannot identify them because it is impossible for me.

Red doesn't exist to me just like depression doesn't exist for most people. We can attempt to describe it in terms that resemble how depression feels, but the words cause no authentic comprehension without first-hand experience. In everyday language, depression is a synonym for sadness. It's something everyone experiences at some point, typically in response to some disappointment.

If you want to actually shine a light on depression or whatever problems may be hiding behind a curtain of ignorance in your life, then you have to do so in the exact same way that I discovered my colorblindness. You have to talk to someone. When you stop burying your emotions and let someone know how you feel, you may be surprised to discover that the rest of the world doesn't feel like they can't get out of the bed in the morning. Other people don't avoid planning for the future because they have lost the ability to see meaning in anything other than simply surviving the day.

My family and I were ignorant of the fact that I was colorblind in the early years of my life. I looked the same. I acted the same. But I was different. Once I started talking about colors with my teachers and parents, my differences started to become obvious. And once we discovered I was colorblind, it became easy to deal with.

I cannot tell you how many people have asked me, "Wouldn't you love to be able to see colors?" My answer always surprises them. "No."

No, I wouldn't choose to be "color normal" even if I could. My students at Scott County High School actually pitched in and bought me Enchroma glasses so I could experience color. It was pretty amazing. I got to see how beautifully blue Georgia's eyes are. I got to see that a tree is two different colors. But since that day, I have only worn my glasses a handful of times. It isn't that I don't appreciate what a wonderful gift those kids gave me. The gift was getting to experience color once. That's enough for me.

See, being colorblind has actually helped me. I truly believe it has sharpened my critical thinking skills because I cannot accept what I see as truth. I have to use deductive reasoning to figure out what I'm seeing. A basic example is that when I see people wearing a University of Kentucky shirt, it may look purple to me. But I've been to enough UK games and heard the chants enough—"What's your favorite color, baby? Blue and White!"—to know that the shirt is most likely blue.

I know that's a seemingly inconsequential example, but every day I have to connect present experience A to past experience B. So when I'm analyzing a complex problem in life, it's second nature to try looking at all the variables to arrive at the most likely conclusion.

The same is true with my mental health struggles. I hid them from the world and from myself for so long. I worked so hard every second of the day partially because it kept me from ever having to think or reflect. If I had taken the time to really look at my life, I would've been forced to accept that I simply was not okay. Today, I would not choose to rid myself of my mental health struggles. They give me empathy for others who struggle. They've given me a heart for every heart that's breaking. They help me accept my own shortcomings and rely more deeply on God. But to get to this place, I had to talk about them. I had to open up. I had to allow other people into my life to be able to discover that they didn't see what I see. They didn't feel what I feel.

I'm colorblind. I struggle from mental health disorders. I'm a manly 5' 7" if I stretch out my neck real long. I like to read. I love sports. Maybe you are some of those things. Maybe you aren't. And that's the greatest gift either of us will ever receive. I don't have to be you. You don't have to be me. We get to be ourselves. So be brave enough to talk to somebody and find out that maybe you aren't like them. Once you do, you'll find that being different isn't as scary as it has always seemed. Give yourself the gift of getting to really be you.

Ignorance Action Challenge

George was born with a fatal heart defect. He was born different. And he was born different in a way that we all would've changed if we could. We all would've taken away his pain. But we also would've taken away what made him special. He changed my life because he was different. I named my daughter Georgia because he was different. You are reading this book because he was different.

- This may seem unrelated, but for each of the following activities, I want you to simply write "yes" if you enjoy them or "no" if you do not.
    - 1) Singing
    - 2) Drawing
    - 3) Dancing
    - 4) Crocheting
    - 5) Creative writing
    - 6) Pottery
    - 7) Woodworking
    - 8) Crossword puzzles
    - 9) Chess
    - 10) Canoeing
    - 11) Hiking
    - 12) Kite flying
    - 13) Scuba Diving
    - 14) Visiting museums
    - 15) Geocaching
    - 16) Gardening
    - 17) Birdwatching
    - 18) Camping
    - 19) Playing a musical instrument
    - 20) Scrapbooking
- Now, beside every option where you answered "no," write how many times you have actually done the activity in question. Write only a number with no explanation.
- Of the activities you said you didn't enjoy, were there some of them you had never even tried? How could you possibly know if you enjoy them if you have never even tried them?
- Here's another example. Write a range of numbers

below that you are confident contains the correct answer. For example, if I asked how many books are in the Bible, you may not know exactly. If you thought the answer was around 50, you may give a range of 35-65. Since 50 is within the range of 35-65, you would be right. All you have to do is give a range of numbers that you are confident includes the specific correct answer. Here's the question. How many countries are in Africa?

I stole that last example from something I saw on Brain Games. There are fifty-four countries in Africa. Did your range include the right answer? If it did, you are probably feeling pretty good about yourself, but you most likely failed the experiment anyway. You probably had no idea how many countries are in Africa so why limit your range at all? Why choose a spread like 40 - 60 when the challenge was to create a range big enough you'd be confident encompassed the right answer. I'd say you would've been pretty confident you had the right answer if your range was 0 to 1 million, but few people choose to do that.

You are overconfident in what you know. So am I. So are we all. It's a human tendency called the overconfidence effect. You don't choose to be this way. Nature made you like this. We have to be overconfident in our knowledge because if we really accepted how much we do not know, then we could not function. We would be paralyzed by doubt with every choice that we made. So your brain makes a decision on what is right based on very little information and runs with it.

Lifestyle change:

This action challenge may have seemed weird. It was different than most in that it didn't address the lesson title in a deep, philosophical way. What I'm trying to show you is that we take so much for granted as truth when in fact it is simply our opinion. Our lives are consumed by ignorance.

Ignorance is not bliss. Ignorance is ignorant. How do you know everyone else experiences failure, loss, and struggles the same as you? Have you actually talked to someone about your real feelings? This is how apathy sets in. We choose to be ignorant to the reality of our world—both our inner self and the lives of those around us.

I really want you to consider this: Why do you have to be good at something to enjoy it? Have you avoided some of the hobbies in this challenge because you may not be great at them? Sing off key. Draw poorly. Write badly. Life is meant to be enjoyed, not conquered.

In the same sense, don't avoid the hard conversations in life because you assume everybody else feels the same as you or because you fear they'll judge you. I would have struggled after George's death no matter what. He was my hero. His loss was devastating to me. But the true leech in my life was silence. I silently assumed his death was my fault. The overconfidence effect allowed me to confuse this opinion with fact even though I had little to no evidence to support it.

If only I had been brave enough to talk to someone. Anyone. If only I hadn't accepted my truth as the actual truth, then ignorance would not have robbed me of over a decade of my life.

Today, destroy ignorance in your life. Choose one of the hobbies listed above and give it a go. Maybe you will try it and hate it. Maybe you try it and love it. The end result doesn't matter. What matters is that you live your life based on actual evidence rather than your assumption of the truth. Once you can enjoy this feeling of real confidence in your decisions, maybe you'll decide to confront ignorance in your inner life as well.

Share yourself with the world. Learn the truth about who you really are: past, present, and future.

Lesson 13: tranquility is real (and you'll never find it looking outward).

[30.] *I have told you these things, so that in me you may have peace. In this world you will have trouble. But take heart! I have overcome the world.*
- *John 16:30*

[1.] *Therefore, since we have been justified through faith, we have peace with God through our Lord Jesus Christ.*
- *Romans 5:1*

True happiness is when what you think, what you say, and what you do are the same thing.
- *Gandhi*

Be at peace. Do not fear the changes of life, rather look to them with full hope as they rise. God, whose very own you are, will deliver you from out of them. He has kept you hitherto, and He will lead you safely through all things, and when you cannot stand it, God will bury you in His arms. Do not be afraid of what may happen tomorrow; the same everlasting Father who cares for you today will take care of you then and every day.
He will either shield you from suffering, or will give you unfailing strength to bear it. Be at peace and put aside all anxious thoughts and imaginations.
- *St. Francis de Sales*

Though the world sees and soon forgets
We will not forget who you are
And what you've done for us
Where you go I go
What you say I say
What you pray I pray
- *"Where You Go I Go" by Jesus Culture*

    Seeing how Sarah dedicates herself so fully to me and Georgia keeps me in awe. It's amazing to see someone love so freely, expecting nothing in return. I don't know if Georgia, or even I, will ever know just how blessed we are that God put Sarah in our lives.
    Before meeting Sarah, I had lived a double life for fourteen years: the me everybody got to see and the me I really was. I tried to project that I was Oz the Great and Powerful, but I was really a scared little man hiding behind a curtain. Sarah was the first person I let see behind the curtain.

Sarah, my love for you helped me to love myself. You made me want to have a real life, not just pretend I had one. God gave you to me. I know this as sure as I know anything. Before Georgia, I used to love everyone in the world. Except myself. I thought that was just fine because I could handle it. That was a lie. I didn't take care of myself, so I couldn't take care of others—not to the best of my ability anyway.

I may be tough, but I am also human, which means I have limits. My disregard for those limits hurt me and, consequently, everyone around me. You gave me the gift of peace. You let me accept my limits. You let me be me.

Being your partner comes natural. We were meant for each other. I can share all of my life with you: the good and, more importantly, the bad. I'm not the best at anything. I just always try my hardest. As a teacher, I had a lot of success. But I had that success because I worked at it relentlessly. As a man and even as a father, I worked tenaciously to be who I thought I should be. Deep down, I have always known I wasn't enough. I masked that with effort and good deeds. With you, for the first time in my life, I don't have to try. I just am. You helped me to accept that I am enough. From our first date until my last breath, you let me be enough.

Still, peace doesn't have a finish line. I don't get to set up my lawn chair in "peace" and take permanent residence. To be honest, I was struggling to write when I started this book. When I wrote *Love is Real*, I wrote from a place of complete ignorance of what a book was "supposed to be." I hadn't written anything that had been read by someone else for over a decade (and even then it was just a paper for a college class).

So I just wrote the truth. As I described in the Author's Note of *Love is Real*, the entire outline for the series was organized as a single book. But, as my editor Jake and I started going through it, I quickly realized that nearly eighty lessons was too much for a single book. So the single book he agreed to edit became two. Then, after another week or so, I realized that nearly 800 pages was going to be too much even for two books, so the one book he signed on for became a three-book series.

Once I settled on a breaking point in the story to serve as an ending for *Love is Real*, I moved from one area I was totally unfamiliar with (writing a book) to more areas I also had no idea how to navigate (marketing, self-publishing, social media, and so on). All of the responsibilities of publishing a book proved to be much more time consuming than I could have anticipated, so I didn't begin the actual final writing process for *Love Redeems* until after the release of *Love is Real*.

Initially, as I wrote this book I was allowing myself to be worried about things way above my paygrade. For example, I was struggling to maintain my voice as an author across the two books. I was having trouble allowing my tone to progress away from my struggle as someone learning to battle mental health disorders in *Love is Real* to expressing authority in *Love Redeems* as someone who has overcome them. I was trying to balance helping the reader develop empathy for my story while also having an authoritative voice so the reader would follow my advice for recovery. Whoa. That gets my brain all twisted up even reading over that. But I was living it. I was writing it.

And I received a lot of positive feedback from the initial readers of *Love is Real,* so there was pressure to make this book "as good as the first one."

Writing this lesson helped bring me back to Earth. I realized I don't have to worry about abstract things like having a voice as an author. All I have to do is tell the truth. Whatever comes out is my voice because, get this, it's my voice. I don't have to worry about what someone else thinks about my voice. It's mine. And I don't have to worry about this book being as good as the first one. Maybe it won't be. Maybe it'll be better.

But, either way, it'll be the truth. That's what *Love is Real* is about. It's what *Love Redeems* is about. It's what *Love >* ___ will be about. It's what my life is about. Write the truth. Tell the truth. Live the truth.

I hope you enjoy the book. I'm writing it for you. I don't want you to throw so much of your life away like I did. I did the best I could do. I told the truth, but the evaluation of the book's worth is yours to make.

All I can control and all you can control is that we live in the truth. Whatever comes with that comes. Peace doesn't come when you receive that promotion at work. Tranquility doesn't set in when you receive an award recognizing your excellence. It doesn't arrive with the birth of a beautiful baby girl.

And it didn't come with marrying my beautiful bride. Peace doesn't lie outside of you. Sarah didn't give me peace. The tranquility she helped me find wasn't in her. It was in me. If you're reading this, your answer isn't in this book. It isn't in a relationship. It isn't in the world. It's in you.

When I started writing *Love Redeems*, I lost sight of this realization for a while. I almost fell into my lifelong traps of writing what would sound good, saying what I know people would want to read. In truth, I have written the vast majority of the *Love is Real Series* through emails to myself. Literally thousands of them. I haven't checked, but I don't think that's how Tom Clancy does most of his writing. Maybe Judy Blume does though. I'll have to ask her.

When I'm not sending myself emails, I'm writing in my journal. Below is a picture of how this very lesson you are reading right now was actually written.

I know you can't read the words in the journal here. That's the point. I could barely read them too.

It's written in fragments. It starts at the bottom of the left page to avoid Georgia's drawing. It goes to the middle of the second page and continues behind her scribbles at the bottom. Then it goes to the top of the right page. And finally it comes back over to the left of that horse-type thing on the first page. (Sorry, Georgia. I didn't mean to disparage your art. That's the best horse/dog/dinosaur I've ever seen.)

As I was typing out this lesson from these scrambled thoughts in my journal, I found my peace again. I just write down the truth as I see it and leave it up to Jake and beta readers to turn that into legible English. That's where tranquility is.

You may like the first book better. You may like this one better. You may hate both. But they are two different books written by the same person trying to tell the truth as he lived it in the moment he was writing. I may get hammered for that by people saying I lost my voice. Or I may get praised for people saying I have a dynamic writing style. Either way, it doesn't matter. Not even one little ounce. Because I'm not writing for a

Pulitzer Prize. I don't think they give those out to people who write their book over their daughter's crayon drawings in their journal.

But that's reality. It's my reality anyway. My life is not the neatly wrapped book you're reading now that has been finely inspected for errors and corrected so that it reads just right. My life is the chaos of trying to understand what in the world I wrote three days ago in my journal because the ink faded off of Georgia's crayon drawing so I can't read it anymore. Life is trying to piece together the flow of my fragmented thoughts written over thousands of emails that aren't in the proper order for story development.

Life is imperfect. It is chaotic. It is often riddled with mistakes and flaws. It is devastatingly painful at times. But it is also beautiful because the seemingly disconnected happenings weave together to make life.

It's beautiful that I struggled to read my writing for this lesson behind Georgia's drawing. It's beautiful that those struggles made me stop, look at her drawing, and remember who I'm writing all of this for anyway. I'm writing because I love her, and I want my life to make her life better. I'm writing because I love you, and I want my life to make your life better.

There is only one path to recovery and that path is found within you. Even when it comes to your relationship with God. The desire to serve Him—to hand over ultimate control of your life to Him—has to come from within you. You have to want it at the deepest part of your being. When you are intrinsically motivated, there is no finish line. We destroy the fallacy of more. We blow up the illusion of better. In every second of every day, in every moment of every activity, I will work to be the best of my ability. I will live my life in a way that honors the life Christ lived for me.

Tranquility lies here because there is no external judgement. It doesn't exist because it doesn't matter.

With Sarah, I slowed down finally. I stopped for a second. And when I did that, I could look inside myself to see what was going on. In my acceptance of myself, finally, I'm working because I get to, not because I have to. I'm loving because it brings joy to my life, not because I have to in order to feel okay. Tranquility isn't in achieving perfection but in accepting imperfection.

Peace isn't found by looking out but by looking in. Looking in and seeing all the broken fragments of your life and the mistakes that have led you to this moment. Tranquility is found when you accept that all those broken fragments stitch together to make you. They make you just as God planned for you to be in this very second. You may be broken, but you are beautiful. You are beautifully broken.

Tranquility Action Challenge

Life doesn't have filters. That's a good thing because those photo filters make you look like a lifeless manikin. Real people have wrinkles, blemishes, and scars—on the inside as well as the outside.

Kintsugi is the Japanese art of repairing broken pottery by mending the pieces together with gold, silver, or platinum. The pieces were once whole, and then they were broken. But someone decided that even though they were broken, they shouldn't be thrown away. They could be whole again in a new way, even more beautiful than they were originally intended to be. Below are a couple of my sketches, but you cannot truly capture the beauty of Kintsugi in black and white. Google it and see the vibrant colors of the gold stitching together what was once broken.

 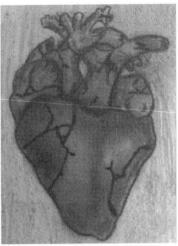

- List some things that have "broken" you in your life.

Most of us spend way too much energy trying to hide these breaks in our life. We pretend we are perfect and nothing hurts us—not now, not ever. What if instead of trying to hide your cracks, you embraced them?

You can't go back to where you were. You'll never be that way again. Your brokenness prohibits that. But that doesn't mean you cannot regain your wholeness in a new way that is even more beautiful than before. The scars of your life tell your story: the life that has been unique to you and has never been replicated before and can never be replicated again.

God loves me, so He gave me the option to choose. He gave me free will. He gave me the option to choose hate, despair, and loneliness. Sarah reminded me that I was making the wrong choice. Sarah reminded me that it is a choice to love. And I choose love.

Lifestyle change:

The unifying theme of this second part of the book is to love freely without expecting anything in return. Often, far too often, we focus that love outward. We praise others for their success and applaud them for their effort even in failure.

Sarah gave me the greatest gift. She let me know that I am okay just as I am. I am broken. And I am beautiful. She helped me to see that. Not only see it, but accept it. Believe it. Live it.

Today, turn that free-giving love inward. Journal five ways that your scars, both physically and emotionally, make you unique and beautiful. You wouldn't be you without them. And you are beautiful.

Part 3: Meet the rest of my family who reminded me of what a gift it was to have known George at all.

Lifestyle change:

    Over 80% of an average person's thoughts are negative. When you think of the survival advantage thinking negatively gave our ancestors, that makes sense. If one person was worried about the dangers surrounding them (and there were lots), then they were much more likely to stay alive. Your 30th great grandpa was on the lookout for danger, so he saw the tiger coming to eat him while the guy next to him spent his last few moments on Earth being mystified by the beauty of the sunrise. Since he survived, he got to pass on his genes to little babies that worried/thought negatively too. If some of his babies weren't so cautious and wary, then they probably became tiger food too. But his prodigy that inherited his tendency to worry about everything that could go wrong would have avoided danger. And so the cycle continued on down to you.

    But I'm guessing that today you don't have a super high chance of being eaten by a tiger. Or ingesting poisonous berries. Or encountering any other imminent, life-threatening situation.

    The benefit of our propensity for negative thought has mostly passed its time. The plasticity of your brain means that it can change. You can reset your brain's tendencies through practicing gratitude. If you practice gratitude every single day on purpose, you are not only making yourself thankful in this moment. You are also making yourself more likely to be thankful in the next.

Lesson 14: Meet my mom, Pat Reid, who taught me gratitude is real (and it is a choice that impacts everything in your life).

Dad and Mom

My brother Alan, Mom, and me on the Myrtle Beach trip described in Love is Real

Sarah, Georgia, and I are giving a peace sign because we're cool. Mom and Dad are not giving a peace sign. You draw your own conclusions about what this says about their degree of coolness.

George in Mom's words:[2]

- George was a very special person. Special, not perfect. I always adored him and Dave. They are as much my sons in my heart as Alan and Adam are.
- George never complained about being sick. We never told him how dire his circumstances were or that he wasn't expected to live very long. But I think that he knew that in some way even as a small boy. George once said, "I wouldn't care to go to Heaven, but I don't know anyone there." Another time, George asked mom [my Mamaw] what they would bury him in if he died because he didn't have a suit. He always liked clothes and liked to look good. He passed this trait on to Alan. Sorry Adam, that must have passed you up.
- When you live with the thought that every event, every Christmas, every birthday, just every day may be the last, it changes how you look at life. That affected not just George but us all. You learned to take nothing for granted, to enjoy the small things. Most of all, to trust in God differently. I am a different person than I would have been if George had not been born with his challenges. Although I would have never wanted my George to be sick, I believe (as George said that God showed him) that his sickness could be used as a blessing. The Bible tells us that ALL THINGS work for the good of those that love Him. It would not be easy for anyone to understand how the sickness and problems that George faced could be a blessing. George said that God told him that due to his suffering, he would share a relationship with Him that would not have been possible for those who had not faced such adversity. That, in suffering, you learn to lean on God in a way that others cannot understand or share. Through this, George changes the lives of those around him. He especially affected Alan and Adam. He groomed them, if you may, to be what he wanted

---

[2] This is continuing "George in their own words" from *Love is Real*. These excerpts were taken from letters written to Georgia about her Uncle George so she could one day know the man who changed all of our lives.

them to be. He worked from the time they were born to lead them to think and act as he would have them to be. He said he was watching out for them so that they would not have "nerds" like he had as role-models. [Author's note: He's referring to my mom who was his role-model.]
- When George got saved, he became a different person in personality and manner. The Bible tells us that when we get saved, we are all changed, but I don't think I have ever seen a bigger change than that in George. George never was a complainer. He always had a good attitude. But there was now a kindness in him that went beyond what can be expressed in words.
- You can make life what you want, for good or bad. Your attitude determines whether you will be happy or resentful. The choice is yours. Always remember that. This understanding is the greatest gift George ever gave me.

Being the gracious person she is, Mom also took the time to be thankful for the other people in her life outside of George in her letter to Georgia.
- Dave - God graced Dave with the personality and gift of compassion and gentleness.
- Dad - God has blessed me beyond measure in making Tim Reid for me. My Tim is one of the most unique, selfless people that I think God ever put on Earth. His gift is the gift of laughter and faith. My life has been full of laughter, and he has given that gift to both of my sons. Tim's bubbling joy and ability to sacrifice himself for those he loves all comes from his deep faith; the ability to look beyond the immediate circumstances with hope.
- Alan and Adam were as much of a gift to George as they were me and Tim. George always said that they were his sons.
- Alan and Adam's personalities are a splice of the characters of Tim, George, and Dave. God took the original molds and perfected them in Alan and Adam. (I admit, modesty is not one of my strengths when it comes to my boys).

Mama there's times where we'll make some mistakes
We know how you've worked and we know how you've prayed
So don't you think twice about where we are tonight
No matter what becomes of us
You gave us enough
Know that we've tried
Home, it might scatter and fade
With time, all things must change
The road, it might take its own course
But I intend, mama, we're still your boys
- *"Mom" by Lucero*

Saying thank you is more than good manners. It is good spirituality.
- *Alfred Painter, French philosopher*

[16] Rejoice always, [17] pray continually, [18] give thanks in all circumstances; for this is God's will for you in Christ Jesus.
- *1 Thessalonians 5:16-18*

Your talent is God's gift to you. What you do with it is your gift back to God.
- *Leo Buscaglia*

    The 80% estimate for negative thoughts definitely understates my mindset during my decade of struggle. For those thirteen years, I had become so fixated on the fact that I lost George that I stopped treasuring the gift of knowing him at all.

    My life kind of just stopped once he died. I kept going through the motions, but I was never really there. Sarah made me want to open my eyes to the goodness in the world again. Once I did, I saw George wasn't gone. He lives on in all of us. All of us are better because he lived. He's gone, but that doesn't erase the nineteen years I had with him. Every single one of those days was a gift.

    When I have a need, it's not Dad I call or my brother/best friend Al. I call Mom. And it's not necessarily because I'm a Momma's boy (although I am 36 years old and she most commonly refers to me as either her baby or her angel). I call my mom because I know she genuinely cares. Not just about me, but about everybody.

    There was a rumor going around that my mom was my main resource during my research for *Love is Real*. Allegedly, she provided lots of invaluable information. I had feared a lawsuit from her after *Love is Real* asking for royalties and punitive damages, but I haven't received my subpoena to appear in court yet. Also, she didn't mention a lawsuit at dinner last night, so I'm going to keep pushing the envelope.

To be safe, let's just say I deserve all the credit for this lesson's material. It's cleaner that way. She probably borrows these ideas from someone anyway. (Can you believe some people will take someone else's concept and try to pass it off as their own? The nerve.) Anyway, let's continue with a concept I completely came up with on my own (but also could have possibly been pulled directly from one unedited text message session with my mom).

I could go through my old texts and pick out countless messages similar to this. I could compile highlights from different occasions to make it more glamorous. But the purpose of this series isn't for you to have a better read. It's for you to have a better life. I want you to see who my mom is every day, who she is when she doesn't realize anyone else in the world will ever know. In *Love is Real*, I quoted Phillips Brooks, who said, "Character may be manifested in the great moments, but it is made in the small ones." For her, gratitude isn't just an emotion. It's a lifestyle.

So, without further ado, here is the material she will be using in her future lawsuit for co-author rights to the *Love is Real Series*. There will be some typos because, like I said, these are the exact texts she sent. I want to emphasize this is my mom on a regular Wednesday. She was the same person the day before, the day after, and every day since. Also, I want to make myself appear to be a better writer than her for my defense team during our court appearance.

- Recounting her emotions after George's transplant:
I remember I had gotten so angry at God, because things were not going the way I expected and wanted for George. When I prayed, I expected results. And it didn't seem he was answering. As we took turns to visit [George's hospital room], *I walked down the hall, and I asked God why he had forsaken us at this critical time. Little did I know or understand, he was moving in a special way. This changes me also. I understood more the plan of God, and that we often don't see or know all he is doing for us. It changed how I looked at all situations.*

- George's death took a toll on us all. Sadly, as much as we loved each other, it seems like most of us struggled through it alone.
When George died, I lost a part of the joy I had. But never was I angry at God or questioned his plan. I don't have any doubt that he had gifted George with more years than he may have been meant to have. I had

seen miracle after miracle. But he had done all he could to make it as easy as he could. He let George see everyone by letting him have those days between the first heart attack when he had been so afraid. George was allowed to make the choice when it was time to go. He was tired of suffering disappointments both physically and mentally.

God sent me home that night so I could not adversely affect George. If I had been there, I would have begged him to go on the ventilator again. I would have fought to not let him go. But that wasn't God's plan or George's choice. I think George would have for me, but to what avail? To have robbed him of time in glory for more time limited here on earth? George had all his work done. God was ready to give him his reward. I don't just believe this, I know it.

- Her message to me about some of my own struggles and self-acceptance:

George shaped us all. We were blessed to know him. But what you need to remember, George became a different man after meeting Jesus as his savior. Tim played a huge part in forming who George was also. Tim's faith helped mold George's own beliefs and faith. God has a plan. He put those two good men in your life to form you. You are the next piece of the plan of God. You have a calling to spread God's love. It is not about being perfect and living a perfect life. That is foolishness. If anyone could live without making a mistake, why did Jesus have to come and suffer?

No, it is quite the opposite. You will mess up. You will make mistakes. Being sinless is not what opens the door to heaven. It is that Jesus' blood covers those sins. He changes our hearts so that we want to do better. And that want helps us make better decisions. Not perfect all the time, but not bad all the time either.

You will share this compassion and the fact that Jesus takes broken things and makes something new. He doesn't take away our personalities and make us different. He takes what is good in us and makes it the dominant part of us. If there are areas that we need to control, he can help us. He is so good, and I love him so. I look forward to going home soon. Seeing George and being able to have peace.

But I want to sit at Jesus' feet and thank him for his plan and blessing for me. If you look at my life, I have been so blessed. I had a good family. I had George, Tim, Dave, Alan, and you. I think you five men are examples of God's best. I have had peace, love, joy and laughter in my life. I am abundantly blessed. No matter what.

She can care so deeply because she has an authentic appreciation of life. Studies have shown that expressing gratitude for what we already have actually makes us happier than getting more.

My life had become a burden. While I was throwing my life away because of shame and regret, there were lots of people out there praying for what I had been given without ever earning: A loving family. A healthy body. The ability to learn. I didn't do anything to earn a functioning heart and lungs. It was a gift. A gift I received and George didn't. A gift I had been throwing away.

Gratitude isn't a singular choice; it is a mindset. It is being thankful regardless of the current circumstances.

If you want a better life, start being thankful for the life you have now. Gratitude breeds more gratitude. The biggest problem most of us face when trying to be thankful for what we have is that we want more. More money. More muscle. More everything. Chasing more is like chasing the horizon. You always seem to be getting closer, but you never get there. "More" is a moving target; one you will never reach.

My mom can be grateful during hard times because she is grateful every day. She practices it without even realizing she is. It's her default mode. It isn't mine. I don't need more stuff—better car, bigger home, more money—but I need to be more as a person. I have always felt the need to be more. As such, I spent most of my life not being grateful.

Happiness doesn't cause gratitude. Gratitude causes happiness. My life didn't get better before I became grateful. I became grateful, then my life got better.

I've had to work to make gratitude a natural component of my life. I've had to set aside times of my day to intentionally practice gratitude. It is becoming more natural, but I still have to be conscious about it.

My greatest test for gratitude came when a student Christian group at MCHS asked me to give a speech on being thankful for their Thanksgiving meeting. This was one month after the lowest day of my life as described in "Lesson 1: failure is real" in *Love is Real*. I gave this speech less than thirty days after I lost everything that mattered to me. I was able to repeat this prayer and still believe its words when I felt like I had nothing.

> *I asked God for strength that I might achieve,*
> *I was made weak that I might learn to obey.*
> *I asked for health that I might do great things;*
> *I was given infirmity that I might do better things.*
> *I asked for riches that I might be happy;*
> *I was given poverty that I might be wise.*
> *I asked for power when I was young that I might have the praise of men;*
> *I was given weakness that I might feel the need for God.*
> *I asked for all things that I might enjoy life;*
> *I was given life that I might enjoy all things.*
> *Almost despite myself, my unspoken prayers were answered.*
> *I am, among all people, most richly blessed.*
> *- Anonymous Confederate soldier, allegedly found on his dead body in Devil's Den after the Battle of Gettysburg*

I was able to believe these words because of my mom. I am grateful to have had a woman in my life who has reminded me again and again and again of the power of thanks. Not just through her words but through her life. I am, among all people, most richly blessed.

Gratitude Action Challenge

6. to the praise of his glorious grace, which he has freely given us in the One he loves. 7. In him we have redemption through his blood, the forgiveness of sins, in accordance with the riches of God's grace 8. that he lavished on us. With all wisdom and understanding, 9. he made known to us the mystery of his will according to his good pleasure, which he purposed in Christ, 10. to be put into effect when the times reach their fulfillment—to bring unity to all things in heaven and on earth under Christ.

- Ephesians 1:6-10

Paul is writing his letter to the people of Ephesus while he is under house arrest. He's been unjustly imprisoned for three years as the Jewish leaders try to have him killed, but he still shows gratitude.

The best fuel for gratitude is to remember our past, the condition from which Christ saved us. Paul would later say in a letter to Timothy that Christ came to save sinners, of which he was the worst. No matter our current situation, we have been delivered from an eternity in Hell when we did not deserve forgiveness.

Thanks is the most commonly used one-word sentence in the English language. Thank you is the most used two-word sentence.

The problem isn't failing to say thanks. It's actually meaning it. We say thank you as a thoughtless reaction rather than a true feeling of gratitude. When we ask "How are you doing today?" to a passerby, it is a rhetorical question. We do not care and do not listen for the response. The person you are asking is equally oblivious to the moment. This is why when someone says, "What's up?" the reply is often "Pretty good." Or, we ask "How's it going?" and the answer we receive is "Nothing much."

You have to actually be present in the moment to be thankful for it. It's hard to be thankful for now if you aren't truly here.

- This was mentioned in *Love is Real*, but you weren't challenged to actually do it. Here, we'll put the concept into practice. The Gratitude Countdown: This is meant to be done with a partner. Your partner says "10" and you immediately respond with something you are grateful for. The more specific the better. For example, I shouldn't just say "Georgia." That's a vague generalization of something I am grateful for. Something specific I'm thankful for would be like "Reading to Georgia at night because I love seeing her imagination work." Once you finish, your partner says "9" and you offer another reason you are grateful. This continues down to one. Then, you switch roles. Although expressing your gratitude to someone else has additional benefits, you can do this on your own if you must. Expressing gratitude in some way is better than not expressing it at all. Take a break from reading, and try this exercise out loud.

    I've done all of these Action Challenges. Rebuilt my life with them actually. But they're not meant to be a one-time action. For a real benefit, you need to incorporate these into your daily life. So I'm going to lead by example. This is an impromptu Gratitude Countdown of my own. I know me. I know I will want to go back and edit this to make it sound better, but I'll refrain from doing so. This is my spur of the moment expression of gratitude.

10) I am thankful for this new career, and I am excited to see the plans God has in store for my life.

9) I am grateful for my mom and the light she has shown in my life.

8) I am thankful to have found Sarah who will be the same type of mother to our children.

7) Thank you God for me.

6) I am grateful for my health and the ability to exercise. I'm in the middle of a Fitness Challenge with our Facebook group. Some of the days have been a bit of a battle to get through. Thank you for giving me the chance to push myself when many people don't get that.

5) Thank you for my editor and for all of the people who have helped this dream become a reality.

4) I'm thankful for the progress Georgia is making in gymnastics. I love seeing her push herself and the toughness she is developing.

3) Thank you for the relationship Sarah and I have. It's amazing to have someone to live life with. From Breakout Games, to puzzles, to video games, to hiking, to just lying around. She makes my life better.
2) I am grateful for the clothes on my back and a warm bed during Winter.
1) I am thankful for my little buddy Bash (my nephew Sebastian). I just looked up and saw a canvas picture of him on the wall. Speaking of gratitude and care, he's the most caring little guy I've ever met. He's a reminder to me of the goodness in people.

I know that wasn't super eloquent. It's not supposed to be eloquent. It's supposed to be real.

Lifestyle change:
Your gratitude isn't just for your sake. It makes the world a better place. I worked with approximately three- to four-thousand kids over my eleven years in education. Most of them said goodbye in some way each day.

One of them didn't say goodbye though. She said the same thing every single day for the entire year as she left class: "Thank you, Mr. Reid."

That seems really simple. Not much different than a normal goodbye, but it really stood out to me. There are some tough days as a teacher. There were days when I stayed late after school the day before preparing a lab and stayed up late that night preparing the lesson plan to be just perfect. Then, nothing goes as planned. The lab messes up. The kids complain. All the work seems like a big waste of time.

But then before she left she'd say, "Thank you, Mr. Reid." On the days when everything went just right—"Thank you, Mr. Reid." On the days when nothing went right—"Thank you, Mr. Reid." Just that small token of appreciation made my work feel like it meant something to somebody.

I've taught Georgia to do the same thing to all of her teachers. When she leaves class each day, "Thank you, ____." One high-school girl's gratitude impacted me. One high-school girl's gratitude now impacts my daughter. Hopefully, my daughter's gratitude will impact some other teacher. Hopefully, that teacher's gratitude will impact her students and her children. And so it continues. But it started with that high-school girl making a simple choice: be grateful and show that gratitude. There will be people who will never know anything about her but will be impacted by the avalanche of gratitude she started.

Today, put into practice a daily expression of gratitude to others. Say thank you and mean it. Start your own avalanche.

Lesson 15: Meet my uncle, Dave West, who taught me humility is real (and there is no greater attribute).

From left to right: Dave, his son Hunter, his wife Beth, and his daughter Laura Beth

<u>George in Dave's words:</u>
- Your daddy [me] and Uncle Alan were two of the closest people on this earth to George, and they will make sure he is a part of your life also. He played a huge part of all of our lives, and I miss him every day.
- When we were really young, I can remember him running when we played. He would run just a little bit, and he would get down on his knees because he would get out of breath. Most of the time, me or Bill Marcum

would carry him on our backs when we played. Between me and Bill, we carried him many miles.
- Your daddy, Uncle Alan, and Bill Marcum were hands down the closest friends that George had. He loved them dearly.
- It's hard to explain, but George was almost like two totally different people in his life, especially to me. He was pretty tough on me when we were small, but when we were in high school George got saved, and he totally changed. He became one of the kindest people that I have ever met.
- Before George's transplant, they made us step out and I remember I started crying. George asked me why I was crying. I can remember him saying, "I will come through this and do better than anyone else has ever done before."
- George's surgery was celebrated in our family like a holiday. We always had his surgery anniversary at Mamaw West's house. Most of our cousins, uncles, aunts, friends, etc. would be there. I would always ask George what he wanted for his anniversary present, which he usually said nothing. For his November 2003 anniversary, I asked him what he wanted, and he asked me to go to church with him. I went to church with George to celebrate his anniversary on November 23rd, 2003, and that morning I rededicated my life to God.
- I asked him what his favorite verse was. He said Matthew 17:20. I asked, "What does it say?" He said, "You look it up". Matthew 17:20 says: *Truly I tell you, if you have faith as small as a mustard seed, you can say to this mountain, 'Move from here to there,' and it will move. Nothing will be impossible for you.* I never forgot this. I told Mamaw West about this after George died, and she had it placed on the back of his gravestone.
- I loved George and miss him very much, but I will see him again someday. I tell people about George all the time and tell them about his life. He impacted a lot of lives during his time on Earth, and he still is.

⁶· *But he gives us more grace. That is why Scripture says: "God opposes the proud but shows favor to the humble".*
- James 4:6

It is amazing what you can accomplish if you do not care who gets the credit.
- Harry S. Truman

But all an empty world can sell is empty dreams
I got lost in the light when it was up to me
To make a name the world remembers
But Jesus is the only name to remember
And I, I don't want to leave a legacy
I don't care if they remember me
Only Jesus
And I, I've only got one life to live
I'll let every second point to Him
Only Jesus
All the kingdoms built, all the trophies won
Will crumble into dust when it's said and done
'Cause all that really mattered
Did I live the truth to the ones I love?
Was my life the proof that there is only One
Whose name will last forever?
- "Only Jesus" by Casting Crowns

    Dave was the only person I can think of who pushed me into teaching. My parents supported me, but their support was universal and unchanging across all of my life. If I had decided to pursue something else, they would have endorsed that too. Dave actually pushed me to specifically become a teacher.

    I thank God for doctors. It's fairly obvious that they are essential to our survival, and their work is crucial. Many doctors become doctors for the right reasons: to help people.

    But that isn't why I would've been a doctor. I would've been a doctor to fulfill a selfish need to repay my debt to George. I would've been a doctor to try to fix my mistake and ease my regret of not sharing my love with him. I wanted to try to become a cardiac surgeon to "fix" people with his heart problem. In doing so, it was my secret desire that I would be able to fix my own broken heart.

    In other words, I had no business becoming a doctor. It wasn't my calling, but I almost did anyway. If nearly everyone else in my life would've had their way, I would have. Except Dave.

He pushed me to be a teacher because he knew I wanted to be a teacher. He knew I was meant to be a teacher. Most of all, he pushed me to be a teacher because of humility. He saw a young man who had a passion for helping kids, and he knew teaching would give me the best opportunity to do so. He didn't see passing up the fancy title of Doctor Reid as some devastating blow.

Humility isn't thinking less of yourself. It's thinking more of everyone else. It's believing every single person matters. When they matter, so do their dreams. And being a teacher was my dream.

I found out a vital truth about writing while compiling Mom's lesson: it is much easier to write when you don't actually write. In fact, just stealing the lesson from someone's text message makes the process a breeze. I got that lesson finished in record time. Maybe that's my author's voice? Just copy and paste text messages? Maybe not? Something to mull over though.

In the meantime, I'm going to continue the thievery in this lesson. Honestly, I'm doing this because, just like my mom's gratitude, my uncle Dave's humility can't be personified in a story. It's who he is as a man. Not only as a man, but as a boy too. It's who he is as a person. He is the most genuinely caring man I know.

Continuing my blatant plagiarism, here is a text mom sent me about Dave:

Often people forget how very special Dave was. He was 17 months older than George. He was so often forgotten and left out; but I never saw bitterness or envy. And he could have. He saw mom spend every waking moment taking care of George while he sat to the side. George received material things that he never had. George had attention that he never had. They had birthday parties for George every year, but never a single one for Dave.

Dave had to work almost all the time while my beloved George taunted him. I always adored both Dave and George. But I knew George was jealous of Dave and was mean to him. Dave wasn't allowed to play with Bill and George unless he did what they said. People [I removed the specific names] *would come in with gifts for George and Bill but would give Dave nothing with him sitting right there.*

God made Dave a very special, compassionate boy and then man. George became a totally different person once he was saved. He became so loving and kind. But he was always that to me, just not Dave. Dave was that way before knowing God; he just became more so with God.

I was charged with Dave's care, and I was just a little kid myself.

If he had been mean or resentful, it would have been so hard for me. But he wasn't. He was a quiet, shy little boy who was so loveable. I think God blesses him because of how kind he was and is.

George needed the love he received from everyone. He needed the gifts and adoration. Even as a little kid, he was fighting to stay alive. A five-year-old can't handle that burden alone.

But a healthy six-year-old needs love too. He needs gifts and adoration too. But Dave didn't get them. Honestly, he was neglected. George consumed all of everyone's attention because everyone knew they may never see him again. If they were with him on a Thursday, there was no guarantee he'd be alive on Friday.

I guess people only have so much love. We only have so much support and attention to give. So as George was heaped with praise and care, Dave grew up in the background.

As much as the world needed George, George needed Dave. He needed a big brother who would love him no matter what. He needed someone who could give him support even though they got very little of it. So Dave loved him anyway. Dave loved all the people who overlooked him anyway.

True humility is not thinking less of yourself; it is thinking of yourself less.
- C.S. Lewis

Now, I don't want Mom to get cocky because I only plagiarize off of her. To keep her ego down, I'll keep my plagiarism rolling with a text message Dave sent me after reading my first book.

I wanted to tell you about something that happened when George was at the hospital the last time. Your book talks about that doctor that came in and talked to George about being a "burden." I thought I had told you all, but this happened before that doctor had even said anything. When George woke up from being unconscious I was sitting beside him. He was still on a ventilator so he couldn't talk besides writing stuff for me.

There was a nurse that came into the room that was going through her procedures of checking everything and normal nurse stuff. She would ask George stuff and he would respond by nodding his head. I never took my eyes off him the entire time. One of the questions the nurse asked (and I quote her exact words and I will never forget this as long as I live), "Do you have a living will?" George shook his head "no." The nurse then said, "That's something you need to think about because that's a hard decision for your family."

George had been watching the nurse the entire time she moved around and asked questions. As soon as she said this his eyes dropped toward the end of the bed. He started thinking about this at that very moment. I have thought about that thousands of times and beat myself up about it.

The thing that has bothered me more than ANYTHING else all these years is that I left the hospital and wasn't there to say goodbye to my little brother. I had been there from the time he pulled into the ER. He wouldn't leave me alone until I agreed to leave [to go to work] *the night before he died. He had talked to me all day about going back to work, and I kept telling him I was fine.*

I finally agreed to go home. I told him I would go home, pack my clothes, and go to work the next day. I told him I would come to the hospital to stay every evening and drive back to forth from work. His exact words were "Deal."

It was for a reason that me and Pat were not there. It was God's plan for us to not be there because I would have pleaded with him to not give up. That would have just extended his sickness and troubles. None of us would have wanted that, and it would've been selfish on our part. His work here was done.

From the same group of text messages, Dave accepting George's death:

Just think of the lives that he changed immediately after he left here. There were people that started going to church and got saved because of him. It's all part of God's plan, and I truly think that.

There is no reason for you to ever spend one more day of your life having regret about his life or his death. That is Satan, the deceiver, that makes us think that way. He wants to steal the work that God has done and make us think negatively with regrets.

George was mean to me until he got saved, but I don't even think of all the mean things or things I didn't get that he did. Even when we were little I was good to him even when he was not so great to me. When Pat and Brian both lived at home I didn't have a bedroom so I slept on the fold out couch in the living room. George slept with me. We played a game every night where we drew on each other's back with our finger and would guess what we were drawing. Of course if I guessed right he would lie and make up something else, LOL, but we both loved that.

There are so many good memories for me. God created George for this world for a reason, but he also created each of us for a reason. He created mommy to care for him, and no other person could have cared for him like her. He gave me patience and forgiveness. God gave us Sis [my mom] *to take care of me. The list goes on and on.*

I still miss George horribly bad, but if he had continued living he would have been worse than ever. If we live to be 90 years old it's just a blink to what awaits us. Just think of the reunion we will all have.

Something to remember every day of your life is if George could have loved us all as much as he did how much Jesus cares about us. We all take this for granted most days, but that doesn't change how much He loves us. I hope you have a great day and I hope to see you all soon.

All these years later, our lives have been rebuilt. We've carried on with life without George. We all loved him. We all loved each other. But when George died, we all lost a part of ourselves. We each held our pain inside. We all faced our troubles alone. We cried alone. We all had regrets when we lost the life that was in large part the foundation of all the rest of our lives. We hurt alone not knowing the cure for each other's pain was to hurt together.

I think we had a misguided idea of what love is. We didn't want to burden each other. We didn't want our pain to become someone else's. And in so doing, we allowed the people we loved to keep on hurting themselves.

Care more about someone else than you do your pride. Humble yourself enough to admit that you can't handle all of life on your own. If you are in pain, tell someone. Tell someone you love so they can love you back. If they think you are strong enough to handle it alone, then they think they should be strong enough to handle it alone. You're not. They're not. We're not. Life is meant to be lived together, in the bad times even more so than the good ones.

Humility Action Challenge

It's an understatement to say I love Georgia. I would give her the world if I could. Saying that, if I could give Georgia one trait, it would be humility. Not strength. Not the grit I am so proud of. Not intelligence or even wisdom.

Humility to realize that everyone matters. Because if everyone matters (no matter what), then that means she will always have to matter (no matter what).

Humility is confused with meekness or self-deprivation. It isn't thinking everyone is better than you. It's thinking no one is better than you, and you are better than no one. We are all the same. We are all beautiful. We are all important. We are all worthy of love.

With humility, Georgia can praise other people's success without having it threaten her own. She can believe others are good without thinking that makes her bad. And vice versa. Just because others are bad, that doesn't make her good. Humility allows you to judge yourself on your own virtue.

Bullies can't use her to feel superior if she refuses to feel inferior. Humility is the basis for all healthy relationships.

- Meg Meeker; Strong Fathers, Strong Daughters

Comparison is the thief of all joy. - Teddy Roosevelt

Jesus didn't just tell us humility mattered. He lived it. Three days before Jesus was to hang on the cross, He was eating with His disciples at what we now call The Last Supper. Jesus got down on His hands and knees and washed the disciples' feet. The Son of God, the eternal King of Kings, washed feet that were filthy from walking wherever these men went. And when He got to Judas—the man He knew would betray Him to His death—He washed his feet. He washed his feet because Judas mattered too. Just as much as the eleven other disciples who would remain faithful to Jesus for the rest of their lives. The man who would betray Jesus and later hang himself out of regret mattered just as much as the men who would become the foundation of the Christian church.

Judas mattered because we all matter. Jesus loved Judas because Jesus is love. Jesus loved Judas because He loves me. Jesus loved Judas because He loves you. Jesus loved Judas because love is love. Every single person on the planet

deserves it. And you are a person on the planet, so you deserve it too.
- I want to do the Gratitude Challenge again, but this time for other people. For all ten expressions of gratitude, give thanks for something good that has happened to someone else. Be thankful for the gifts others receive.

10)

9)

8)

7)

6)

5)

4)

3)

2)

1)

Lifestyle change:
    Gratitude and humility are the key components to a joy-filled, loving life. The Gratitude Countdown this time should've been equally easy (or equally difficult if you're not accustomed to practicing gratitude) to the one focused on you in the previous lesson. I'm going to break the rest of this *Lifestyle Change* into sections because you will need different adjustments to your life depending on which category you fall in.

- Both Gratitude Countdowns were hard to complete:
    Most likely, gratitude isn't a common expression in your life. That's okay. If we're honest, most people are going to fall into this category. We're so busy with things that "have" to get done that we lose focus on less important things like, you know, enjoying life.
    I was in this category. You may be like me. I had to put daily gratitude practices into my schedule to be sure I'd actually do them. You already have The Gratitude Countdown, so keep trying it. In *Love is Real*, I shared four gratitude questions that Georgia and I do each night. As a reminder, they were:

    1. What have you done to make yourself happy today?
    2. What have you done to make someone else happy today?
    3. What has someone else done to make you happy today?
    4. What have you learned?

One final suggestion would be trying a gratitude practice called Person, Pleasure, Promise. This exercise is more structured and can make it easier to get a grasp on gratitude (if you are a beginner like I was in this whole being appreciative thing). You will journal three things you are grateful for: one person, one pleasure (something you enjoy), and one promise (something you are hopeful for/excited about).

- The Gratitude Countdown for yourself (last lesson) was harder:
    Humility isn't about lowering yourself under people. It is

about raising everyone else up to you. That means for humility to have any real meaning, you must first value yourself. Humility is accepting that I matter just because I matter. And if that's true for me, then it has to be true for everyone else.

Allow yourself 15 minutes of "me time" every day this week. It doesn't matter what you do, as long as it doesn't involve playing on your phone, being productive, or helping someone else. Realize that you matter even when you aren't giving to others.

- The Gratitude Countdown for others (this lesson) was harder:

Either you don't feel enough thanks for the blessings of others, or you just aren't aware of them. Either way, that's probably an indication that you need to become more invested in the well-being of people in your life.

The next conversation you have with a friend, refrain from talking about yourself. Truly listen and be invested in what they are saying. If you want to be happy, learn to celebrate the successes and joys of others. If you're only happy when good things happen to you, then you are going to be unhappy for a good portion of your life (because nobody has only good things happen to them).

- You easily completed both challenges.

If thoughts of gratitude flowed for yourself and for others, then you've got two of the most important attributes to a healthy life (gratitude and humility) down. You just keep doing you.

Lesson 16: Meet my cousin, Bill "Stumpy" Marcum, who taught me that transformation is real (and it can happen whenever and wherever you decide).

Top Image - March of Dimes Walk 2004 - We had about 40 people come to celebrate George's life. From left to right: Dave, Bill, Me, Little Adam (Bill's son) on my shoulders

Left Image - Bill's family - From left to right: Bill's daughter Leeann, his son Adam, Bill, and his wife Tracy

George in Stumpy's words:
- When trying to think of a single story about George, I find it almost impossible to do. I get half-way through one story, then I think of another. There were so many great times, so many laughs, so many adventures.
- When I started playing football, George was the manager and would wear my number on the sidelines. I remember how hard I played to try to impress him.
- Of all the memories I have, there is one thing I have no memory of at all. In a world filled with crumbling and complaining, I never remember a time of George complaining about being sick or the cards he was dealt in life. Even the many times I visited him while he was in the hospital, he was always the same. Always laughing, always outgoing, always making the people around him feel better.
- On George's final hospital trip the night before he passed away as I was leaving he told me he loved me. For the first time, I told him I loved him. I'm glad I got the chance to do that. Never be afraid to tell someone you love them. I was later told that his dying words were to tell Bill, Adam, and Alan to get saved just before lifting up his hands and heading off into Glory. Those words did not surprise me. Even near death, he was thinking of others more than himself.
- Throughout my life, I have met a lot of people and made a lot of friends, but I believe in a person's life there is only one best friend. George was mine. I hope someday that you or I can have half the impact on another person's life as George has had on mine. I know that I will see him again as he left this world with a testimony that he had put his faith in Jesus, and since then, I have done the same. I can only imagine the great times, laughs, and adventures we will have as the ages roll on. I hope you are there with us. I love you.

39. One of the criminals who were hanged there was hurling abuse at Him, saying, "Are You not the Christ? Save Yourself and us!" 40. But the other answered, and rebuking him said, "Do you not even fear God, since you are under the same sentence of condemnation? 41. "And we indeed are suffering justly, for we are receiving what we deserve for our deeds; but this man has done nothing wrong." 42. And he was saying, "Jesus, remember me when You come in Your kingdom!" 43. And He said to him, "Truly I say to you, today you shall be with Me in Paradise."
  - Luke 23:39-43

Everything changed when I fell on my knees
Everything changed when your love rescued me
From reckless and wild to faith like a child
I was never the same
Everything changed
  - "Everything Changed" by Zach Williams

26. I will give you a new heart and put a new spirit in you; I will remove from you your heart of stone and give you a heart of flesh.
  - Ezekiel 36:26

It was just another summer night
Had to be the last thing on my mind
When love broke thru
  - "Love Broke Thru" by TobyMac

12. For I will be merciful toward their iniquities, and I will remember their sins no more.
  - Hebrews 8:12

    Bill and George were first cousins. More importantly, they were best friends. From childhood to George's death, Bill was as close to George as anyone. The only other two people who would be in contention for that title would be Alan and me, but George looked at us as his sons. He looked at Bill as his equal. That's saying a lot actually—to be George's equal. George was the wittiest, funniest guy I ever knew. And Stump was his running mate.
    Their shenanigans are the source of some of the funniest stories of my life. But the reasons they're so funny are the same reasons that it's probably best I leave those stories out of this book. Not sure they're quite appropriate. Let it be enough to say that Bill brought joy and laughter to

George's life. And George repaid him with the same. As Bill said, hopefully most of us have many people we call friends. Not everyone has a best friend though, someone they can depend on in any situation, at any time, and at any cost. Bill was George's best friend in every sense of the word.

Growing up, Al and I were with Dave, George, And Bill constantly. They groomed us so that, as George lovingly put it, we wouldn't have nerds for role-models like he did. This meant Al and I had to constantly earn our keep. We would always be on call to go fetch drinks, chips, and whatever else. We were kids who were always with teenagers so we were at their beck and call.

At least Al was. They seemed to always make him do all the running while I kicked back. I had things figured out. I once told Mom, "If you do it slow and do it wrong, they don't ask you to do it again." Genius.

Although Alan and I both idolized George, Alan is much more like him than I am. Of all the people in my life, I am probably most like Stumpy—the good and the bad. He is a fierce competitor, driven beyond reason toward success in whatever he pursues just like me. You can essentially think of Stump as an older, less agile, less handsome, and less charismatic version of me.

We were all a crew, but for the last several years of George's life, Bill and I were probably together more than any other combination of the group. Dave was married and living in another city. George had a serious girlfriend he spent a lot of time with. Al graduated high school and was a singer in some rock bands so he was off doing his own thing a lot. That left me and Bill. During that time, I practically lived with Stumpy.

Our similarities allowed us to play video games for about eight hours straight every night and never grow tired of them. From Triple Play '99, EA Sports NCAA Football, and most every Madden game over a ten-year stretch, we would keep a paper copy of our win-loss records for trash talk. At the end of each game, we would each have to flip into "4th-quarter mode" (which, for a true gamer, is the highest level of intensity and focus).

My external initiation of this flip would be to drink a Mountain Dew and his would be to put in a dip of Skoal. Looking back, I'm not sure Doing the Dew six-to-ten times a night was all that healthy. Neither was dipping two cans of Skoal. Maybe flipping the switch would've been better kept in a metaphorical sense? Hindsight is 20/20, but in this case it seems like regular ole sight should have sufficed too.

At George's death, he did what he did during his life—he loved people. He singled out the three people who were closest to him in his life for his greatest request: Alan, Stumpy, and me. This was the last thing George ever said to me directly. They had given him an additional dose of morphine. It was kicking in and George was losing his grip on reality as his life slipped away. Alan and I were in the room, but I'm not sure he realized that anymore.

Tell Adam, Alan, and Bill that if they ever want to see me again, they have to get back in church.

He died a few minutes later.

I had followed every single thing George told me my entire life. I fulfilled every single request he ever made of me. (I still technically fulfilled his request to fetch stuff. I just fulfilled it slowly. And intentionally got the wrong stuff. It was his choice to not make those requests to me again.) I modeled everything I was and everything I did around the person I thought he wanted me to be.

I did everything he ever asked of me except this last, most important request. I ran from that statement for a long time. I had spent my entire life in church every Sunday morning, Sunday night, and Wednesday night. I had averaged attending church three times a week up until George's death. I only went to church maybe twenty or thirty times over the next thirteen years. I went when it was socially expected of me and when my absence would've been disrespectful to Dad. On Easter, I would be in the pews. On Dad's Pastor Appreciation Days, I was there. Basically, besides that, I wasn't.

I couldn't go to church. I couldn't have a relationship with God. If I did, I'd have to be honest with Him. I'd have to talk about how I had failed George, and I couldn't talk about that.

Instead, I decided to never talk to God. I had wholeheartedly resolved to never truly go to church again. Not in the real sense anyway where I would open myself up to God's presence. And I had accepted the fate for my soul that came with that decision.

My hesitance to ask for God's forgiveness was born out of the personality traits Bill and I share. George once told me, "I can't believe you went down looking." He had been talking about a youth baseball game. I took what he was saying to heart. I promised myself to never go down looking again.

And I hadn't. I had worked for every inch of life. I had refused to give up. I had battled back against every obstacle. I had gotten what I deserved because I earned it. I was fast because I ran until my body started shutting down. I threw up thirteen times in a single track meet from exhaustion. The only reason I didn't throw up a fourteenth time was that the track meet ended, and I went to the hospital for dehydration. I bench pressed twice my body weight because I stayed in the gym and would sometimes get out of bed in the middle of the night to do more push-ups. I was a great teacher because I worked nearly eighty hours a week.

I earned my shame too. My life's purpose was to be George for the world, but I failed to be George for the one person who really needed it—him. He needed love just as much as the rest of us. I would wear my shame as a punishment for failing George who had never asked us for anything but had needed us nonetheless.

I earned my punishment. I earned the burden of being destroyed mentally. I earned my depression. I earned my anxiety. I earned the alcoholism and the arrests. I earned my pain. At least, that's what I thought. So I would bear it.

Like I said earlier, I've never met anyone quite so much like me as Stump. I've never met anyone with the resolution to never fail and to be self-reliant in all things like him. As a reminder, he's older, less handsome, less charismatic, has less of the "it" factor, and probably smells worse. Besides that, we're the same. That's why seeing his change was instrumental in me being able to make a change of my own.

Stump loved George just as much as I did. Stumpy was just like me. But he wasn't. He wanted to see George again some day just like I did, but he was strong enough to admit he needed help. He was brave enough to accept he needed a change in his life, so he fell on his knees in his house and asked Jesus to forgive him of his sins.

A church building is often referred to as God's house. In reality, God is everywhere. He is in the church, but He is also with you right now. God's household is not a building, but a group of people. It's us.

> [9.] *If you declare with your mouth, "Jesus is Lord," and believe in your heart that God raised him from the dead, you will be saved.*
> *- Romans 10:9*

Stump and I were two guys who were just the same. Both of us loved someone we lost. Both of us knew what we had to do if we wanted to ever see that person again. Stumpy did something about it while I ran from it. Stumpy had his entire life changed from the inside out. He had the love and joy of Christ permeate into all areas of his life and into all his relationships. Stump got up off his knees and joined a church. His family followed him. Stump went into prisons to tell people who had messed up that Christ loves them anyway and that change was possible for them too.

I drank. I ran. And I destroyed my life. I threw away a third of my life to the lie that I had to make the change myself. It took my love for a little girl named Georgia Lynn Reid for me to become brave enough to make the same change Stumpy had over a decade before.

You don't have to "get your life in order" first. You don't have to quit drugs first. You don't have to stop cheating on your family first. You don't even have to go to church. He's there with you with arms open wide asking you to come to Him. I wasted so much of my life trying to earn God's grace. I tried to fix all the mistakes I had made. I tried to buy back my life. I thought if I helped enough people—if I did enough good—maybe then I could be saved. Maybe then I'd be worthy of His love.

We make salvation much more difficult than it really is. Believe in your heart Christ died for your sins and was raised from the dead with power over the grave. Confess with your mouth that Jesus is Lord and has forgiven your sins. Done.

Transformation Action Challenge

Change can be scary. Especially when you've tried before and failed. But it is real.

- Describe a positive transformation you have seen in someone else's life.

It really does kill me to write this, but I know that some people had to leave the question above blank. You do not have an example of someone bettering themselves. You don't have an example of someone making a real change and seeing that change last. If you were one of those people, please list three people you love.
1.
2.
3.

Lifestyle change:

Some of you have been influenced by the change you've seen in others. Follow that person's lead.

If you haven't seen anyone make a positive transformation, it is very likely that those three people above have not seen it either. If you want them to have a positive change in their lives, they have to believe it is possible. Maybe you aren't even sure change is possible for you. On our own, you're right. Maybe if you are a drug addict, you will always be a drug addict. Maybe if you are a cheater, you will always be a cheater.

But not with Christ. True transformation doesn't happen with you trying to change yourself. It happens when you let Christ do the change for you.

Christ didn't come to save the righteous. He came for the sinner. He came for me. He came for you. Be the person who shows others that change is possible.

It can be tough to ask for forgiveness when we don't deserve it. We've all had the value of earning what you receive drilled into us. Well, you can't earn this. You can't earn God's grace. It's free.

Transformation is real. My dad was a man who was afraid of the dark with a violent temper. He's now the most joyful person I've ever met. George was bitter and bordering on being cruel to his brother Dave in his resentment of Dave's health. George became the most loving person I've ever known. Stumpy was self-reliant and manic. He's now fully reliant on Christ in his life. I was broken. I was never going to be enough. Now I am whole. None of us earned it. We all just asked for it, and it was given to us freely.

You don't fix your life so you can come to Christ. You come to Christ so He can fix your life. No lifestyle change could ever be greater. If you need a change in your life, fall on your knees and ask Christ into your life. Your life could be different this very second. Not tomorrow. Not next Sunday when you can get to church. Right now. Wherever you are. Choose to make a change.

Lesson 17: Meet my brother, Alan Reid, who taught me the truth is real (and what you remember becomes what happened).

Alan's family - From left to right: my nephew Sebastian "Bash", my niece Piper, my sister-in-law Mary Beth, and Al

Alan and me at Tough Mudder 2015

Me, George, and Alan on the Myrtle Beach trip described in Love is Real

> *George in Al's Words:*
> - George always included me and Adam in everything. Every day with George had the potential to turn into an adventure.
> - George was one of the funniest guys I've ever known. Even in some of his sickest times, he would have us cracking up.
> - He would never let us win at anything. If it were a contest or game of any sort, and we happened to win (an unbelievably rare occurrence), then we definitely earned it. This was just one of the countless things that was so awesome about George. He never treated me or Adam like little kids, because he really didn't think of us as just little kids. George always treated us like we were one of his closest buddies and more. George was one of the very best friends Adam and I will ever have, but he was so much more than that. He honestly had an impact in molding every single thing about us. If you look at either of our likes or interests, they were without a doubt something George would have liked as well.

[7.] *I have fought the good fight, I have finished the race, I have kept the faith.* [8.] *Now there is in store for me the crown of righteousness, which the Lord, the righteous Judge, will award to me on that day—and not only to me, but also to all who have longed for his appearing.*
- *2 Timothy 4:7-8*

[32.] *Then you will know the truth, and the truth will set you free.*
- *John 8:32*

In "Lesson 7: goodbye is real (and one day it will be forever)" from *Love is Real*, I talk about the turning point of my life: George's death. That singular moment altered my trajectory from a high-achieving, loving person to a shell of a man clinging to the remnants of who he once was.

On July 14th, 2004, the world was robbed of George Alan West. And it was my fault. George died thinking his health struggles made him a burden on his family. He died thinking we would be better off without him. At least, that was the version of his death I chose to live with and nearly allowed to destroy my life.

I never spoke to a single person about that night in Myrtle Beach. I never shared any of the countless other times I almost got the courage to tell George how much I loved him either. I never told anyone that the secret to my ability to seemingly never give up was that I had already given up a long time ago. I gave up on my life beside the deathbed of my hero.

One day soon after I returned from the mission trip discussed in the ending of *Love is Real*, I opened up with someone about George's death for the first time. I was going to go on a quest for forgiveness. I was going to tell every person who loved George that it was my fault they lost him. I was going to ask for their forgiveness so I could forgive myself.

I started this long tour of admission with my brother Alan. He is my best friend. His relationship with George most closely mirrored mine. George was his hero too. He was one of the six people at George's deathbed. I felt like I robbed Alan the most. Like me, he didn't know a world without George. From our births, our lives had been centered around becoming who we thought George wanted us to be.

I told him about the doctor who made George feel like he was a burden. I admitted to him that I had the chance to save George's life that night in Myrtle Beach. I exposed my guilt. My undeniable, unforgivable guilt.

It was quiet for a few seconds that felt like a few minutes after I spoke. In my mind, Al was trying to process his devastation. His response was simple and something I couldn't have predicted if I had a million guesses. Alan simply said, "That isn't what happened."

He was ending my quest as soon as it started, so I tried again to make sure he knew the truth. "What do you mean that isn't what happened? I was there. I know. That's what happened."

Alan told me George had suffered another heart attack and refused to be put back on the ventilator. They gave George morphine to put him to sleep. Even then, George's willpower was too strong. The normal lethal dose didn't kill him even in his weakened state. He stayed with us a little longer.

I remembered all of that. I remembered that he could barely die even when he was trying to. I had used this as the basis for believing that if I hadn't robbed George of knowing how much he impacted my life, then he would have made the choice to go back on the ventilator. And if he hadn't chosen to die, then he wouldn't have. I remembered his strength and used it as evidence that I had killed him.

I had lived my life thinking I was the only person in the world who knew the real story of how we lost the gift of George Alan West. I only shared my secret with the bottle. And I shared frequently and deeply. I shared enough to be arrested six times for alcohol related offenses. I mentioned that in passing in an earlier lesson, but this is the first time I've actually shared that truth completely. Five of those arrests were for being non-functionally drunk in public (once a year from 2005 to 2008 and again in 2013). When I say non-functionally, I mean I was a completely incoherent zombie. One of those arrests was for peeing on the floor of a crowded bar. I have no recollection of it happening.

    I drank to the point of no return nearly every night for a decade. In truth, I should've been arrested hundreds of times. I destroyed part of my brain to the point that I struggle with memory. I laugh it off as forgetfulness, but the truth is my drinking irreversibly damaged my brain tissue and short-term memory.

    My last arrest came with my DUI on my final night of drinking on July 27th, 2018. Six arrests. That number could have and should have been seven, but on one occasion the cops feared I may die from alcohol poisoning if they took me to jail. They took me to the hospital instead.

    I drank to escape the reality of who I was and what I had done. But I drank because of a reality that was actually a lie. A lie I believed because I never told anyone what I perceived to be the truth. No one ever had a chance to refute it. I made up my own reality where I was the villain. George died. It had to be someone's fault. I decided it was mine.

    I fought so hard to cover up the truth of my failure that I ended up becoming a failure in truth. I was a failure for over a decade because of one mistake. One mistake I wouldn't share because I didn't believe good people made mistakes. At least not mistakes that cost the people they love their lives.

    I remembered all the tears during George's death. The tears I was responsible for. I remembered all the pain. I remembered all the regret. So, in my life, that was what happened. I destroyed my body, spirit, and mind for over a decade because I knew that was what happened.

    But Alan's recounting of George's death didn't end there. It went past what I had remembered. Al started reminding me of things I had once known but had forgotten. He recounted the truths I had suppressed to the point that I wasn't choosing to ignore them anymore. I did not know they existed. They were no longer a part of my reality.

You don't remember what happened. What you remember becomes what happened.
- John Green

    The truth had become buried so deep beneath my shame I couldn't find it on my own. Alan opened my eyes to the fact that George's death wasn't a time of desperation and loss. Not for him anyway.

Like I said in *Love is Real*, we had our entire family in the St. Joseph's waiting room for three days before George died. The majority of them left because George was doing better. They went home for one day—and only one day—to get a change of clothes and put things at home (work, family, etc.) in order.

God chose that day for George to go. Up until that moment, I had believed that a calloused doctor who I hated with a venom that infiltrated everything in my life had caused that decision. I was wrong. God chose that day because that was the day He had predestined from George's birth to take one of His greatest gifts back home.

In the end, there were six of us left at the hospital. George's mom and dad, Alan, Alan's wife Mary Beth, me, and George's ex-girlfriend who had come to visit him that morning. God selected us six. He chose George's mom and dad to be there because they had been there for him his whole life. He chose them for George. God picked Al for me. He knew I'd need him to tell me the truth years later. Mary Beth was there to be Alan's source of strength. George's ex-girlfriend only came one day—that day. God let her be there because George still loved her and wanted her there. She was the closest thing to a "normal life" he had ever known.

And God chose me to be there. He chose me so He could choose all of you. He chose me so George's story wouldn't end with our family. He chose me so you'd be reading this at this very moment in your life.

I knew George's death was drawn out as we waited for the morphine to take him. All I remembered happening during that time was my longing to beg him not to go. I remembered standing hopelessly by the bed as George's life—and in a sense mine—slowly drained away. But Alan didn't just remember the few extra minutes George lived on Earth. He remembered what he did with them.

Alan reminded me that George told us to thank the people in his life for what they had done for him. Not just the major characters in his story like his family and best friends, but literally everyone. George went through a list of people who had made his life better—nurses, doctors, acquaintances—and told us to make sure they knew what they meant to him. He did the same thing in his death that he had done in his life: love. Love every single person.

Alan opened my eyes to the truth that George's life was dictated by his health. Every second of it. Everything he did (and everything he was never able to do) was impacted by his health problems. His health struggles had a hold on his life, but they didn't get to have a hold on his death. He chose to go. The heart attack didn't choose. George did. Maybe for the first time in his life, he got to make a choice independent of his health.

My memory of what happened was fragments of the truth. I remembered the pain. I didn't remember that the pain was mine, not his. George wasn't sad. He was happy. He had finished his race. He had kept the faith. His battle was won. I needed him to stay. He was ready to go.

I could've avoided all of the drinking, the brain damage, and all of the arrests if I had been strong enough to admit I was weak. Brave enough to admit I was scared. I could've believed the truth so much sooner if I had allowed someone to tell me it.

I didn't really talk much with anyone else after that talk with Al. I didn't share with anyone else directly besides Sarah. The first time anyone else knew about my struggles was reading *Love is Real*. My parents, my family, my friends. They found out about my depression, anxiety, and alcoholism when you did. Here is a text I got from Mom as she was reading.

You are correct; he chose. He may have not made the choice if that heartless doctor who did not know George and his family hadn't placed this additional burden on George. But what Satan didn't want you to know was that this wasn't a decision he had made in one day. He had been thinking about God's plan for him for much longer. When he had asked me not to have him placed on the ventilator again he had already been making his plans.

He had been having night terrors that he was going to die alone. That he would have a heart attack and not be able to call out to Mom and Dad.

But that is not how he left this world. He left with those he loved around him. Those that he needed to be with him. He told me that you and Alan were the closest things he had to his own sons. He wanted to be able to encourage you to serve God. He loved Tiffany still, and he would have wanted her there. This book and the message to be open and talk to those you love to share your burdens and pain are so important as you can see from just the prep for your book. If we had all shared, you may have not had to carry the heavy load that led you to depression and alcohol.

George was never able to run. His artwork you saw in *Love is Real* was born from his practice as a child. While other kids ran and played, he drew. The pictures you saw of him wearing ninja armor or an army outfit as a kid were because he dreamed of running. My dad tells about racing Dave and Bill with George on his back. He remembers George laughing and taunting Dave and Bill. "Come on, boys. You all can run faster. Don't give up."

He said when Dad ran with him on his back, it felt like he was running. George dreamed of being strong. George dreamed of being healthy. George dreamed of running. That dream came true on July 14th, 2004. He never ran a day on Earth. He's run every day since. I'm pretty fast. I bet he's pretty fast too. He probably thinks he's even faster than me. I guess one day we'll just have to see.

The thing Al told me that sticks out the most is pretty simple. He said, "He didn't flinch." Maybe that above all else encompasses who George was. He faced death like he faced life—with courage, faith, and love. I think George knew death was just one more battle he had to fight. One last battle. George was stronger than death just like he had been stronger than life. But George's power isn't what prevented him from flinching. He didn't flinch because he was marching forward with Christ in his heart. And this battle, like every one before, had already been won.

Alan gave me the gift of truly seeing the last second I ever spent with George. His race was finished, and God let me see him cross the finish line. George could've chosen to stay. He chose to go. And he did so joyously. The very last thing George ever did on Earth was reach his hand up to Heaven, smile, and die.

[31] But those who hope in the Lord will renew their strength. They will soar on wings like eagles; they will run and not grow weary, they will walk and not be faint.

- Isaiah 40:31

Truth Action Challenge

I loved George. I still love George. I was so focused on the time we lost that I forgot about the time we had. I never told him directly just how deep my love for him was, but he knew. I have a book I made in third grade about him being my hero. Here is the shadow box with a lot of our memories and excerpts from that book.

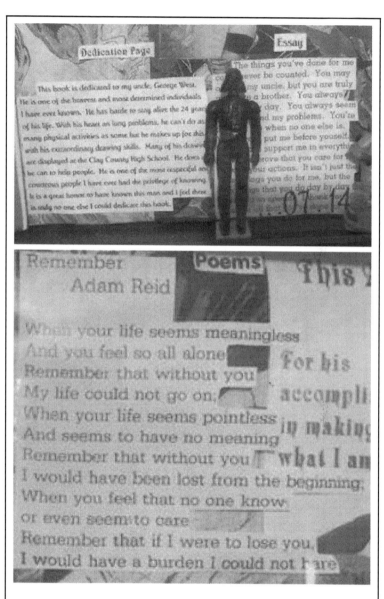

It's okay if you can't read those. They're not my greatest work. Give me a break. I was nine. The point is George knew. Maybe I never told him directly, but he always knew.

I started my quest to live in the truth by finally opening up to my brother. I wanted to acknowledge my wrongdoings and have others see me for who I truly was even if that meant their opinion of me worsened. Much of my shame was misplaced and unwarranted. But maybe your truth isn't redeeming. Maybe you did something awful. Maybe there is no alternate version of your story. But the truth is the truth. It's the only path out of the darkness. In the truth, you can live in the comfort of knowing you are no longer prisoner to your mistake.

Many of us are living with secrets because we fear the repercussions of people knowing the truth. What so many of us fail to see is the damage that living our lie does not only to us but to everyone around us. We live as less than ourselves. There is always a distance between us and the people we love because we can only let them so close. Our lives are dictated by secrecy and fear. Numbness covers our lives and our relationships.

Let someone in. Give them the opportunity to love the real you.

- The fear that you'll be judged and ridiculed is real. I'm not minimizing that. There may be real life consequences. But there are real issues that come from hiding the truth too. We can become so accustomed to the pain and struggle that comes from our silence that it can simply become a part of our lives. We carry the weight of the world so long that we no longer recognize its presence. So lay it out plain and clear. Below, describe everything you believe could happen if you expose hidden truths in your life. Be honest about everything—the good and the bad—that could happen both from telling the truth and unburdening your silence.

Lifestyle change:

For me, when I did this exercise, I learned that the truth wasn't as scary as I had thought. I had been focused on the negative in my life for so long I had become blind to all of the love around me. I was in such deep pain that I let it shroud the reason the hurt could penetrate my life so deeply. I admired George. I've written a book about him, and it's still not enough for you to understand who he was. In the end, Winnie the Pooh understood the truth of my life better than I did.

How lucky am I to have something that makes saying goodbye so hard.
- Winnie the Pooh to Piglet

Instead of living in so much pain that he was gone, I've started living with gratitude that he was ever here at all.

Take one step. That's it. One small step toward the truth today. My step was talking with Alan. It shined a light on a redemptive truth for me. Even if it hadn't, it would've been worth it to open up. You can't seclude a part of you in some dark closet and expect the rest of your life not to be impacted by it.

Start with the list above. Maybe share that list with someone else. Or if it's too personal to reveal to those in your life, talk with a therapist. No matter how bad things could get, at least they'll be true. At least your life will be real.

Part 4: Meet me, again, who has learned through all of his failure that...

Lifestyle change:
    I spent the majority of my life trying to be more. Trying to be better for the people I love. Trying to make up for past mistakes. Trying to be enough. Just trying to be anything besides me.
    Self-realization requires self-acceptance. We all have a unique purpose. Our individual talents and gifts are prerequisites for fulfilling this purpose.
    The only way you will ever become who you were meant to be is to be you. Celebrate your good. Try to improve your bad, but accept the bad does exist. Just be you. All of you. Somebody out there needs you to be.

Lesson 18: suffering is real (and I thank God for that).

Always forward. Never Backwards.
- Pops, Netflix's Luke Cage

I won't look too far ahead. It's too much for me to take.
But break it down to this next breath,
This next step, this next choice is one that I can make.
So I'll walk through this night,
Stumbling blindly toward the light.
And do the next right thing.
And, with it done, what comes then?
When it's clear that everything will never be the same again, then I'll make the choice to hear that voice
and do the next right thing.
-"Next Right Thing" by Anna in Frozen 2
(I bet I've seen this movie more times than you. Definitely not by choice though...)

The way I play, most people we play against, they ask me the same question during games. "Bro, how do you not get tired?" I say, "I do get tired, but I don't stop when I'm tired. I stop when I'm done."
- Oscar Tshiebwe, UK basketball player

During suffering, a man may remain brave, dignified, and unselfish or in the bitter fight for self-preservation he may forget his human dignity and become no more than an animal.
- Foreword, Man's Search for Meaning

"Man's inner strength can rise above his outward fate."
- Viktor E. Frankl, Man's Search for Meaning

    You're reading a book series based largely on my suffering, but most of that suffering is past tense. It's told with the certainty of reprieve from a man who has come through to the other side.

    I know that's not the case for many of you. You are suffering right now. In this very second, your life is in shambles.

    Notice how much of this series is based on verses, quotes, prayers. I didn't look all of those up to write this book. I found them all during my struggles and in my refusal to give up.

I found them where you are right now: in the darkness. Your life may be devastated. You may be broken. But you are still here. You are alive. That's all you need to have another chance.

You have a choice. You can choose to quit. Or you can choose not to. You can choose to be defeated. Or you can choose not to be. For a long time, my greatest accomplishment was just surviving. Just having the resolve to say I may give up one day, but that day won't be today.

When you're in the valley, the mountaintop can seem impossibly far away. If you want to see change in your life, your focus can't be on the ultimate goal. It can't be on the mountaintop. The possibility of ever reaching that peak can seem so distant and slim. Sometimes, when you are truly suffering, the only thing that matters is the next step.

The first night Georgia was gone, I knew my life could never be good again. I wholeheartedly believed that. I could never be whole again. But I could take one more step.

After my DUI, my fears were fulfilled. I was destroyed. The only thing I had left—my good name—was now gone too. I had nothing left but shame and regret over a life wasted. I could never be whole again. But I could take one more step.

Carrying Georgia's car seat into school was the most humiliating time of my life. I had never wanted to do anything or be anyone besides that little girl's Daddy. And I had failed at even that. One more step.

Not being able to breathe and constantly feeling like I'm going to gag. One more step.

Flinching instinctively every time I drove by a semi-truck on the interstate out of fear of what my subconscious would drive me to do. One more step.

So take a step. One step. That's it. One step away from where you are. One step away from the source of your suffering. You're not trying to take a leap all the way to recovery. Just one single step.

Once you've taken that step, you're one step closer to the mountaintop.

Then take another one. And another one. Keep taking one more step. Maybe one day you'll give up. Maybe one day you'll lay down and quit. Maybe one day you'll be defeated for the last time. But today, decide to keep going. Keep taking another step.

Someday that next step will be the one that places you on the mountain top that seems so far away today.

Suffering Action Challenge

Suffering in and of itself is meaningless. We give suffering meaning by the way we respond to it. I thank God for my suffering. It gave me the chance to be more than I am.

The world can't see the difference my suffering made. I was always going to be who I am on the outside. I had resolved to be this person since my very first memories. I was going to be George for the world. Maybe not to the level he was, but I would do my best to mimic him.

But, ultimately, God used George's death to teach me more than his life. He let me love him so much that it broke me. He let me be empty so I could have empathy for others who are broken..

Still, I understand it's hard to see the meaning of your suffering when you're in it.

There was a transport of a specified number of prisoners to another camp. It was understood that this "camp" would be the gas chambers...
Although the officers selected the numbers, there was a "sort of self-selecting process going on all the time among the prisoners"...
On the average, only those prisoners could keep alive who, after years of trekking from camp to camp, had lost all scruples in their fight for existence; they were prepared to use every means, honest and otherwise, even brutal force, theft, and betrayal of their friends to save themselves. We who have come back, by the aid of many lucky chances or miracles—whatever you may choose to call them—we know the best of us did not return.
- Passages describing his time in concentration camps from Viktor E. Frankl's Man's Search For Meaning

It's hard to see the meaning of such suffering. A lot of times, we may never personally see the purpose of our pain come to fruition. I know Viktor E. Frankl wasn't thinking of me, a man he would never meet, during his time of imprisonment. But his book changed my perspective on life in many ways. The insights he gained from suffering made my life better along with the lives of millions of others who've learned from his writing.

- If you are suffering, don't look for the greater meaning. The fact is, you may never know. And even if you do, it will almost certainly be found in retrospect. Below, describe the reason why today won't be the day you give up.

Lifestyle change:

Ultimately, that is the only way through suffering. To refuse to merely sit still and wait for the passage of time to carry your pain away. If you lay down, when you finally get back up you'll still be in the same spot. Your troubles will still be with you.

Today, take a step. One step. If you are a recovering addict, maybe tomorrow will be the day you succumb to your addiction. But not today. If you are struggling with thoughts of suicide, not today. If you are battling an eating disorder, not today.

And when you make it through today, pick the same mantra back up tomorrow. I recently celebrated 1,000 days of sobriety. When I woke up surrounded by drug addicts and women beaters, I couldn't see today and my life beyond my addiction. All I could see was the destruction of what was once a promising life.

But that day, I resolved not to take a drink. I could face my problems sober and deal with what may come for a single day. I did the same thing the next day. And I did the same thing this morning. And I'll do the same thing tomorrow.

Find the spark that gets you through today—whether that spark is inside you, in the lives of people you love, in this book. But you won't find it lying down. You won't find it by giving up.

So take a step.

Lesson 19: self-control is real (and knowing what you are running toward).

¹². It teaches us to say "No" to ungodliness and worldly passions, and to live self-controlled, upright and godly lives in this present age.
- Titus 2:12

¹³. No temptation has overtaken you that is not common to man. God is faithful, and He will not let you be tempted beyond your ability, but with the temptation He will also provide the way of escape, that you may be able to endure it.
- 1 Corinthians 10:13

Every temptation is an opportunity to do good. Every temptation is a choice to do the right or wrong thing.
- Rick Warren, A Purpose Driven Life

    Refraining from drinking for over 1,000 days isn't my victory. I could stop drinking and still be a drunk. I did it before. Lots of people are doing it right now. Avoiding their addictions all while remaining an addict.
    Self-control doesn't start with your actions. It starts with your heart. The Pharisees read Moses' law against murder and felt righteous because they had fulfilled that commandment on the surface. Their actions supported what the law said, but they let anger and hatred into their hearts. Their actions lived by the law. Their hearts eventually led to the murder of Jesus Christ.
    We miss the intent of God's word when we read His rules for living without trying to understand why He made them. Jesus emphasized if the act is wrong, then so is the intention.
    People crumble before temptation every day. I did too. For a long time. After every mistake, we swear to ourselves it will be the last time. After I'd be black out drunk and trying to fight my best friends, I'd wake up to say never again. And I would hold to that resolve. Until I didn't.
    The problem is we allow ourselves to slowly wade out into deeper waters. We never consider our danger as the water climbs past our knees and up to our torso. We may start recognizing we have a problem as the water gets up to our shoulders, but most of us still assume we're safe. It's not until the water is at our chin and we're on the verge of drowning that we begin to try swimming back to the safety of the shore.
    Some of us make it. Many of us don't.
    The problem isn't the temptation itself but our mindset concerning temptation. It's not about the act—it's about the desire. It's not about resisting temptation with the body—it's about resisting it with the soul. If

you allow the seed to be planted in your heart, it is inevitable that it will eventually germinate in your life.

My self-control wasn't about stopping drinking. Honestly, that was the easier part for me. This is why the most important element to recovery is to slow down and really reflect on your life. Look at yourself from all angles. I won the fight against alcohol for fourteen months before my divorce. A lot of people patted me on the back for my self-control. I did too. I was an alcoholic, and I quit drinking. So I win. I was in control of my life.

I was wrong. I thought I had defeated alcohol, but I hadn't. I had resisted drinking, but the true enemy was still at my heart's gate. I lost the fight because I was swinging at the wrong enemy.

I gritted my way through avoiding the action but not the thought. The thought remained. The more I tried to fight it, the deeper it entrenched itself in my psyche. I was still an addict in my heart.

Pride was my greatest temptation. Not alcohol. I had been able to stop drinking, but I had done so through willpower. I stopped by avoiding alcohol and situations where people were drinking. I was moving away from alcohol, but I wasn't moving toward recovery. I had no ultimate goal other than "don't drink."

After the divorce, I started drinking again. I started drinking again because I had proven to myself that I was okay. My actions said so. I had stopped for fourteen months. That's plenty of evidence. I was fine. I could drink. And I got a DUI nine months later.

You may be leaving behind a past with mistakes you no longer want to make. You may be doing a great job at abstaining from your vice. Maybe you've made it a day. Or a week. Or a month. Or years. But if you remain fixated solely on your problem, you're never going to win. Even if you resist the temptation for the rest of your life, you will have lost because, in your mind, you've always been captive to that temptation. It's still dictating your thoughts, your actions, and your life.

I didn't drink, but I was still a drunk. A drunk where it mattered the most: my heart, my mind, and my soul. A prisoner not to alcohol but to shame and avoidance.

Maybe drinking isn't your temptation. Maybe it's food. Maybe it's your image. Maybe it's pornography. Don't kid yourself that you are winning the battle by resisting your urges for a while. You cannot will your temptations or your desire for them away. I promise you, if you expect yourself to never lust again, you are wrong.

Even Sarah, who is married to the manliest man to ever be a man (looking like a little-old-man-boy is manly, right?) will sometimes have lustful thoughts. I know. Shocking since she has this to come home to.

Even though she is the best person I've ever met, she's still a person. That means she still lives in the flesh and will face temptations.

> *^{27}"You have heard that it was said, 'You shall not commit adultery'; ^{28} but I say to you that everyone who looks at a woman with lust for her has already committed adultery with her in his heart.*
> *- Matthew 5:27-28*

So, who can be sinless? Who can avoid experiencing temptation in their heart?

Nobody. Not me. Not you. Not Sarah. Not your husband or wife. Not your kids. Not your pastor or priest. Maybe you can resist the sins people see, but what about the ones behind closed doors?

God considered Job the most righteous man on earth not because of his actions but because of his heart.

> *^{31} "I made a covenant with my eyes not to look lustfully at a young woman.*
> *- Job 31:1*

He made a covenant with himself not to avoid the action people see but the desire that leads to the sin.

I can be around people drinking today and know without a shadow of a doubt that I won't give into my temptation to drink. Yes, I may want to. So what if that desire comes? I have a pretty strong desire to be the running back for the Philadelphia Eagles too. But even if they let me, my 150 lb. body would be broken in about half a second. A part of me wants to challenge the biggest, most athletic men on the planet. A much smarter, more rational part of me knows that's not the best choice.

I may think, "It's been almost three years. I'm okay now. My life is different. I can drink again." But I won't believe those lies. Maybe they aren't lies. Maybe I could drink responsibly now.

But I'll never know. I'll never know because I'm not willing to risk it. I'm not willing to risk Sarah. Or Georgia. Or myself. I love all of us more than I love drinking.

The answer for me resisting lustful thoughts isn't in willpowering myself to never have another. The answer is in loving Sarah and Georgia more. And I include Georgia equally. Dad always told me that a man that cheats on his wife does so on his entire family because he betrays the trust of them all. Our chances of redemption aren't in wanting the world less. It's wanting Christ more.

> *When there is no law, there is no sin, because people cannot know that their actions are sinful unless a law forbids those actions. God's law makes people realize that they are sinners doomed to die, yet it offers no help. Sin is real, and it is dangerous. Imagine a sunny day at the beach. You plunge into the surf; then you notice a sign on the piers: "No swimming. Sharks in water." Your day is ruined. Is it the sign's fault? Are you angry with the people who put it up? The law is like the sign. It is essential, and we are grateful for it—but it doesn't get rid of the sharks.*
> - *Life Application Study Bible, Romans 7:9-11 explanation*

The law spoken of above is not man's law. It's God's law. It is the instruction left for us to live by. Often people get confused and believe living this law equals salvation. Nothing could be further from the truth. There are three myths to self-control that we must accept are false.

1) Knowledge of the rules is the answer.
2) Self-determination is the answer.
3) Becoming a Christian stamps out all sin and temptation.

Wrong.
Wrong.
And Wrong.

Just as my body is more than an ear or a heart, my being is more than my desires and thoughts. I control my desires. My desires do not control me. I don't run from my temptations. Instead, I do the exact opposite. I acknowledge them completely without shame or judgment.

Equanimity is mental calmness even during difficult situations. It is the mindset of just being okay. Being okay when you feel bad. Being okay when you feel good. It allows us to accept each moment just as it is. It encourages us to step into clear or muddy waters with equal confidence. It strips the power away from our addictions because we look them directly in the face. We move all around them and study them. We don't flinch or tense up when they come around. We become used to them. There are times I am not tempted to drink. There are times when I am. And I'm okay during both of them.

It's smart to avoid temptations early in recovery. For me, I didn't go around people who were drinking for a few months. But relying solely on avoidance robs you of part of your life. I missed being around friends in social gatherings. I didn't want to take away a part of their life they had no problem with. They can drink responsibly so they should be allowed to.

Eventually I had to face the problem. The real problem. Just refraining from drinking was like just cutting a weed for me. The root remained so it eventually grew back. You have to remove the root of your temptation and replace it with feelings and actions that honor God. You have to move past the symptoms to the cause.

We have a misconception about what self-control really is. Resisting temptations isn't achieved by a further reliance on self. In fact, it's the opposite. To gain self-control, you must give up control all together. That seems to be contradictory, but even Jesus Christ gave up control when being tempted.

> *[1] Then Jesus was led by the Spirit into the wilderness to be tempted by the devil. [2] After fasting forty days and forty nights, he was hungry. [3] The tempter came to him and said, "If you are the Son of God, tell these stones to become bread." [4] Jesus answered, "It is written: 'Man shall not live on bread alone, but on every word that comes from the mouth of God." [5] Then the devil took him to the holy city and had him stand on the highest point of the temple. [6] "If you are the Son of God," he said, "throw yourself down. For it is written: "'He will command his angels concerning you, and they will lift you up in their hands, so that you will not strike your foot against a stone." [7] Jesus answered him, "It is also written: 'Do not put the Lord your God to the test." [8] Again, the devil took him to a very high mountain and showed him all the kingdoms of the world and their splendor. [9] "All this I will give you," he said, "if you will bow down and worship me." [10] Jesus said to him, "Away from me, Satan! For it is written: 'Worship the Lord your God, and serve him only."*
>
> *- Matthew 4:1-10*

Satan tempted Christ with the same decoys he uses as lures against us: pride and power. Jesus was not half-God, half-human. He was fully God while still being fully human. He felt the temptations of the flesh just as strongly as you or me. But unlike us, He had the power to make His problems disappear with the snap of His fingers. But He didn't. He resisted Satan's lies by casting him away as a human. He did this to set an example of how we are to resist temptation. Jesus walked out of the desert victorious not because of His strength, but because of His unrelenting reliance on God.

Christ showed us the way. We don't avoid succumbing to temptation through willpower or personal strength but through leaning on the one weapon in the armor of God—the Word. When we truly fall in love with God and long to live by the instructions He left us, we are finally prepared for the battle. Not because of our strength but because of His.

Sin promises what it cannot deliver. That next drink won't make it better. The next time you bury your feelings in food won't make them go away.

In *Love is Real*, I introduced the Great Exchange: "Are you willing to trade what you want the most for what you want right now?" My victory isn't what you see. It's what you don't. It's closing my eyes at night and being able to go to sleep. I finally overcame my addiction not by wanting to drink less but by wanting to live more.

Self-control Action Challenge

- What is your greatest temptation? What most often makes you be less than you are?

- Describe your history with this temptation. What mistakes has it caused you to make? Have you ever stopped before? How did you do it, and for how long? Where are you with it right now?

Today, I am nearly three years sober. Obviously, the time I have resisted alcohol is longer this time, (34 months > 14 months) so objectively I'm doing better. But I've only been sober three years because that's all the time that has passed since my DUI and my last drink. Ten years from now, I'll be thirteen years sober; twenty years from now, I'll be twenty-three years sober.

I can make those declarations with absolute certainty because I'm not running away from alcohol anymore. I'm running toward a new life. I'm running toward peace, joy, and love.

Let's try a new way of facing your problem. It's one thing to say, "Love Jesus more. Love yourself more." It's quite another to actually put that into practice. Let's try to gain a deeper understanding of your issues. Strip away the uncertainty. Rip away the mystical nature of it. Understand it so you can understand how to overcome it. Don't run from your addiction. Face it.

First off, don't grit your teeth and bear through your temptations. Resisting in that way is a fallacy of a win. You've won the battle, but you've lost the war. Willpower alone is not enough because these urges will attack again and again. One day they'll attack when you're not ready. They'll surface when you don't have the strength to resist them.

For a lot of us with addiction or impulse-control issues, that one loss is all it takes to start the avalanche. One slip, and we fall back into old habits. You have to find the root of the addiction, face it, accept it, and overcome.

Here's the method I learned from Jeff Warren's meditation (the same guy who taught me RAIN from the anxiety lesson). It's called SURF. The next time you feel your urges start to surface:

- **S**top - Literally stop. Recognize the urge that is happening. Be with it.
- **U**nderstand - Don't run from it. Don't grit your teeth and brace yourself until the urge passes. Face it. Understand it. See what the temptation feels like and where in your body you sense it. Part of the problem is fear of the unknown. Know your enemy.
- **R**elax - Temptation has a bell-shaped curve. It comes on quickly, but it fades as well. Instead of going up

and over the roller coaster by giving in to the temptation, do the opposite. Breathe deeply, relax back into your normal state.
- **Freedom** - Enjoy the satisfaction of having the temptation arise and resisting it anyway. You may never outgrow temptation. I haven't. Not entirely at least. But you can enjoy not being a slave to your addiction. My addiction is still here, and I'm still here too. My greatest victory isn't that my alcoholism vanished. It's that it didn't vanish, but I have chosen to be greater than it.

Lifestyle change:

Maybe you have physically overcome your temptations. Maybe you haven't. The key to finding true victory over them is the same though. You may have left your mistakes in the past physically, but you could still be in the same spot as the addict who's using every day.

You have to overcome your temptation in your mind and in your heart. Shake the dust off of your boots. Leave the past in the past. Move toward your future.

Nah. That's not enough. Originally, that was the end of this lesson. But I'm writing this additional section as I proofread the book. You've wasted so much time bogged in the past and in your mistakes. Don't waste another second. Don't just move toward your future. Run toward it. Sprint toward it. This second. I usually give a time range to do these lifestyle changes. Not for this one. Right now. Don't go to the next page and continue reading. Stop. Put the book down. Go take the first step toward your new life. Stop moving away from your past and start moving toward your future. Stop running from your mistakes and start running toward your redemption. Stop running from who you were and start running toward who you are.

Lesson 20: setbacks are real (and they are inevitable).

15. I do not understand what I do. For what I want to do I do not do, but what I hate I do.
— Romans 7:15

I've stood on this stage night after night
Reminding the broken it'll be alright
But right now, oh right now I just can't
It's easy to sing when there's nothing to bring me down
But what will I say when I'm held to the flame
Like I am right now
I know You're able and I know You can
Save through the fire with Your mighty hand
But even if You don't my hope is You alone
They say it only takes a little faith to move a mountain
Well good thing a little faith is all I have, right now
But God, when You choose to leave mountains unmovable
Oh give me the strength to be able to sing
It is well with my soul
— "Even if" by MercyMe

Remember how far you've come, not just how far you have to go. You are not where you want to be, but neither are you where you used to be.
— Rick Warren, A Purpose Driven Life

I am not fully healed. I am not fully wise. I am still on my way. What matters is that I am moving forward.
— Yung Pueblo

Last night I dreamed that I'd been drinking
Same dream I have 'bout twice a week
I had one glass of wine. I woke up feeling fine.
And that's how I knew it was a dream
It gets easier, but it never gets easy
— "It Gets Easier" by Jason Isbell

I have not failed. I've just found 10,000 ways that won't work.
— Thomas Edison

The answer for your life isn't in wanting the flesh less. It's in wanting Christ more. But what happens when you experience a setback? What if you have a relapse into your temptation whether it be drugs, alcohol, pornography, eating, or whatever form temptation takes? You are human after all. There was a reason Jesus had to die on the cross. He was perfect. We are not. So how do we keep one mistake from becoming two? One snowflake from becoming an avalanche.

This was perhaps my biggest area of growth. I was so obsessed with perfection that anything less than that was devastating. If I made one mistake, I was destined to make more throughout the day. My psyche was destroyed. I had no restart button or safety net.

The world needs people to be real. The caricatures of perfection society creates (and we so desperately try to adhere to) not only hurt us but everyone who knows us. I believe self-control is real and attainable, but I don't want to paint the picture that this will be easy. Self-control isn't a one time decision. It's a decision you'll have to make over and over and over again. Just because you make it today doesn't mean that you can face your temptations with any less resolve tomorrow.

That can be a daunting realization. The battle is never over. Not in this life anyway. It can feel like we aren't allowed to make a mistake. That's the exact opposite of the Gospel.

I still have dreams that I've been drinking. It's been three years, and I still sometimes relive all the things I've done to people. I relive the shame to the same depth every time I wake up from these dreams. For the first few seconds I'm awake, the dream was real. I've done it again. I've hurt people again. I've disappointed myself, my daughter, my wife, my family, and most importantly, my God. I still wake up some mornings and reach to feel my nose to see if anyone hit me while I was blackout drunk the night before.

I could look at these dreams as nightmares. I could look at them as punishment, but I choose not to. They are my reminder of what I once was but no longer choose to be. They are my assurance that I'll never go back.

You will be challenged your whole life. Often, your setback will mask itself in good intentions so that you succumb to them without even realizing it. Recently, I was reading my Bible (specifically the book of Ecclesiastes). I was taking notes as I read like I always have. This, in itself, is a positive act that allows me to slow down and gain a deeper understanding.

But, for the first time, I was doing it for the wrong reasons. I was reading my Bible as a textbook, researching for this chapter. I was looking for content instead of reading the Bible as it was intended. It's God's love letter to us. It's supposed to be read intently and taken in with not only our minds but, more importantly, with our heart.

But I was abusing it. I was abusing it for my own purposes.

I will never drink again, but I will have setbacks in my true addiction: pride. I had fallen back into the same personal shortcomings I've struggled with my whole life. Ironically, it was during research for a lesson about setbacks. God has a sense of humor.

I am writing this book for you, not me. The purpose of this book is to love you. But, for a couple days, I let it be about loving me. "How can I make this sound better? How can I sell more books? How can I prove to everyone how great I am? The first one did pretty good. This one has to be better."

The "what" wasn't bad (using information from the Bible). The "why" is where I faltered. No one in the world but me would have known this. But if I would've allowed it to continue, all of my work would've been hollow. It would've been the difference in this book fulfilling my life's purpose (using my personal struggles to spread God's love) or the book becoming another mechanism for self-reliance and pride. The thin line between these two extremes was as simple as my mindset while writing.

I asked God for forgiveness. And I am now asking for forgiveness from you too. I am sorry for valuing myself more than you. Please, forgive me.

I could've held onto my mistake. Punished myself for screwing up, again. Belittled myself for being vain and self-serving, again. I could chase the past I cannot change. Or I can accept my failure and move toward what the future holds.

I wish I didn't have to tell you about messing up. Vulnerability isn't really very fun. Admitting my weaknesses isn't enjoyable. But that's how you overcome setbacks. You accept you are more than a single action. You are more than what you do. God loves you when you live righteously in Him. He loves you when you don't. Our longing to live in a way that honors Him is not a prerequisite to earning His grace. It's a response to what He's already done.

I realized that God allows us to feel pain for a reason: to protect us. God uses many things to show us what to avoid, and painful consequences often teach us lessons quickly.

- Tony Dungy, Quiet Strength

Tony's adopted son, Jordan, has a genetic disorder that doesn't allow him to feel pain. That may seem like a blessing because his little boy will never be hurt physically. It's a curse.

Cookies are good. But in Jordan's mind, if they're good out on the plate, they're even better in the oven. He will go right in the oven when my wife's not looking, reach in, take the rack out, take the pan out, burn his hands and eat the cookies and burn his tongue and never feel it. He doesn't know that's bad for him. Pain sometimes lets us know we have a condition that needs to be healed. Pain inside sometimes lets us know that spiritually we're not quite right and we need to be healed and that God will send that healing agent right to the spot.
- Tony Dungy speaking at an Athletes in Action breakfast

Don't punish yourself for your setbacks. Embrace them. Accept them as God's reminder of your need for Him. If you never feel the pain of mistakes, you may never get back down on your knees and talk to God. He can become so easy to ignore when everything is going right.

But what about the pain that isn't curable? What about setbacks to your life that can never get better? The times where you know your life can never be the same again.

Tony didn't only speak of his son Jordan. He also talked about his oldest son, James. His son who had committed suicide at age 18. I talked about this in the "Vulnerability Action Challenge." I said someone needed to hear about his failures, not just his success. Here are those someones.

"I met a guy the next day after the funeral. He said, 'I was there. I heard you talking. I took off work today. I called my son. I told him I was taking him to the movies. We're going to spend some time and go to dinner.'"

Tony's son's organs were donated. Just like someone's decision to donate their organs provided George with the heart and lungs that gave us ten more years with him, James' decision impacted another life and another family.

"We got a letter back two weeks ago that two people had received his corneas, and now they can see."

Through this terrible situation, fathers were influenced to reconnect with their sons. People regained their vision. And most importantly, a girl who had known James came to know the Father.

"When I saw what happened at the funeral, and your family and the celebration and how it was handled, that was the first time I realized there had to be a God. I accepted Christ into my life and my life's been different since that day."

It's great that you are working on self-control. It's great that you are trying to live for God. People need to see that. They can be inspired by it. Lives can be changed by it.

Maybe it won't be your successes that change lives but your failures. You have to accept that God loves you anyway. People need to see that God loves you anyway. Then maybe they can believe that even though they've failed again and again and again, God can love them anyway too.

Setbacks Action Challenge

Often the harshest condemnation comes from within. We self-sabotage because we feel like we deserve it.

If my struggle is food, I punish myself by overeating after a mistake at work.

If my problem is alcohol, I binge drink after an argument with my spouse.

It's the negative vortex I discussed before. I think poorly of myself so I feel poorly about myself. My feelings lead to self-destructive behavior which makes me think and feel even worse.

We have to alter the way we think about ourselves and our mistakes. One mistake doesn't have to become two. Our mistake can be a chance for growth, not another validation that we cannot overcome our problems.

- Think of any mistake you've made recently. Describe it below. What led to you making the mistake? How did you think, feel, and behave in the immediate aftermath?

Lifestyle Change:

Change your viewpoint on your mistakes. Instead of focusing on the pain, focus on the reason why we feel pain in the first place: as a warning sign. Allow your setbacks to open your eyes to what led to the mistake. Don't fixate on the fact that you are human, and you have made a mistake. Fixate on the fact that you are a human, so you need to rely on God. Shift your attention to how you could be living in a way that ensures you rely on God more deeply.

That's a lot easier said than done though. It's one thing to say not to beat yourself up over mistakes. It's another to actually refrain from it when you've spent your whole life responding to failure this way (which is true for the vast majority of us.)

So this lifestyle change won't be about what you do when you make your mistake. It'll be about what you do right now. Say out loud, "God loves me."

That's it. That's the secret to not allowing one setback to result in a complete backsliding in your new life. God loves you. He loves you when you don't mess up. He loves you when you do. So when you mess up again, let the first three words out of your mouth be, "God loves me." If you believe those three words, then you can use the pain of your mistake as God intended it—to keep you from making the same mistake again.

Lesson 21: God's love is real (and we are Barabbas.)

Sometimes my love looks like the sea
And you just cannonball
But either way I hope that you jump right in
Let my peace you can't comprehend take over your heart
Take over your thoughts
I'm invisibly aware
Just try to receive what I give free and know
Where you go I am there
...
When you run away
Know that I'll keep pursuing your every mistake
Just know that I'll use it to break others' chains
When you testify of what I've done

— "I am" by Judah

He said you're undeserving cause I know where you've been.
I have a record of your life when you were bound by sin.
I know your darkest secrets that you would never tell.
What makes you think
you don't deserve a place with me in hell.
I heard the old accuser and this was my reply;
"You're right for all the things I've done, I sure deserve to die.
My righteousness is filthy rags. My goodness is unclean.
There's only one thing I can say to what you've said to me.
It's under the blood. Oh praise His dear name.
I'm not what I used to be. My life's been changed.
Not shackled by sin and shame. It's already gone.
I'm happy reminding him. It's under the blood.

"It's Under the Blood" by The Inspirations

[21] *So I find this law at work: Although I want to do good, evil is right there with me.* [22] *For in my inner being I delight in God's law;* [23] *but I see another law at work in me, waging war against the law of my mind and making me a prisoner of the law of sin at work within me.* [24] *What a wretched man I am! Who will rescue me from this body that is subject to death?* [25] *Thanks be to God, who delivers me through Jesus Christ our Lord!*

— Romans 7:21-25

¹¹· When the Pharisees saw this, they asked his disciples, "Why does your teacher eat with tax collectors and sinners?" ¹². On hearing this, Jesus said, "It is not the healthy who need a doctor, but the sick. ¹³· But go and learn what this means: 'I desire mercy, not sacrifice.' For I have not come to call the righteous, but sinners."

- Matthew 9:11-13

I wanted to be George. It was a plan I'd made before I even realized I'd made it. It was a plan that led me to fighting a bully five straight days in kindergarten. My entire life was built around that one goal: be George for the world.

That was my plan. It wasn't God's. God's plan was for me to be his opposite. God planned on me being me. I was meant to complete the circle to create the full picture of God's love. God's love is for people like George. It's also for people like me. And you are somewhere in that circle too.

If George was meant to show the world how good we can all be in spite of our circumstances, I believe I was meant to be his counterpart. Not to show our similarities, but to highlight our differences. George kept his strength while I lost mine. God loved us both. George lived the life I want for Georgia while I lived the life I'm trying to protect her from. And God loved us both.

Paul wrote thirteen books in the New Testament. God chose Paul to be the world's greatest missionary. We both know about Jesus today largely because of Paul 2,000 years ago.

But Paul wasn't always Paul. He was originally Saul. As Saul, his job was to hunt down Christians and have them put to death, a job he enjoyed. He took pleasure in witnessing the stoning of Stephen. He hated Christians and they feared him. Yet God chose Saul to become one of the most influential Christians to ever live. God chose Saul to be His voice to the world not because of his goodness but because of his lack of goodness.

¹⁵· Here is a trustworthy saying that deserves full acceptance: Christ Jesus came into the world to save sinners—of whom I am the worst. ¹⁶· But for that very reason I was shown mercy so that in me, the worst of sinners, Christ Jesus might display his immense patience as an example for those who would believe in him and receive eternal life. ¹⁷· Now to the King eternal, immortal, invisible, the only God, be honor and glory for ever and ever. Amen.

- 1 Timothy 1:15-17 (Paul writing to his protégé Timothy)

If you haven't picked it up from reading this series, Jesus came to save sinners of which I am the worst. I believe that to be true in the deepest part of my soul.

But, as I'm writing this, I wonder how many of you are thinking the same thing: "If you only knew ME, you'd know that I am in fact the worst. The most unworthy of love."

So many of us are trapped in these false shells of kindness toward others while we harbor hatred and resentment toward ourselves. All have sinned and fallen short of the glory of God. You're not the worst. Neither am I. It feels like a lie to write that even still, but it isn't. The remnants of my self-deprecation remain to the point where it still feels blasphemous to say that I am not the worst person to ever live. The truth is I'm just one of the many unworthy souls the only worthy man to ever live died for. And so are you.

I believe God meant for me to tell George's story. And for me to be able to tell George's story, I had to tell mine. I believe that was His design for you to see both, side by side. To see the person you want to be in George and perhaps the person you are in me.

Together, George and I complete the circle. We connect the ends of what mankind can be—the best and the worst. And God loved us both. You are good. Or you are bad. And God loves you the same.

You've never fallen too far that He can't pick you back up. You've never gotten too lost that He can't find you. We have the idea of salvation completely backwards. We think, "I'll fix my life and then I'll be able to have God save me. I'll quit drinking. I'll quit lying. I'll quit cheating. Then, God can love me."

You don't fix your life to give it over to God. You give your life over to God so He can fix it.

And even if we are able to accept we are saved by God's grace alone, it's then easy to misconstrue how we are meant to live the rest of our lives

There is no greater example of God's grace in the Bible than Barabbas. It was customary that each year at the Passover Festival a Jewish prisoner would be released back to the people. There were extreme tensions and volatility between the Jews and the Roman government that ruled over them. This act was a token of concession by the Roman government toward the Jewish people to appease them. When Jesus was sentenced to death, Pilate gave the people the option of who was to be released: Barabbas the rebel or Jesus Christ the Messiah. They chose Barabbas.

There's a sermon by Judah Smith titled *"We are Barabbas"* in which he details who Barabbas really is: me and you.

How many times have I stood on that platform with Jesus and Pilate while I am Barabbas? They start to take my chains off, and I say, "No. No. I deserve this. I deserve the guilt. I deserve the shame. I deserve the consequence. I deserve it."
Jesus seems to look at me and say, "No, son. Let me have it. Let me have your sin. Let me have your pain."
"No, God, I did it to myself. I deserve it. My marriage won't make it. This is what I deserve. I deserve divorce. I deserve sickness. I deserve poverty."
"NO!"
"God, I'm so ashamed."
"Give me your shame."
"But God what if I do it again?"
"I'll still be here."
"Oh, God, I don't want to hurt You. I love You. I don't want to do this anymore."
"Give me your sins, son"
...
Okay. And I give Him my sin. I stand in this empty space of forgiveness and acceptance while Jesus walks off to the cross that I deserve. I see Him. I see Him walking to the post to be whipped as I stand a free man. All the attention is turned now, and I feel the love of God saying, "Go, Son. Live your life. I'll pay the price."
Where did we get off thinking we were going to set ourselves free? It's still Jesus. It'll always be Jesus. It'll never stop being the power of Jesus. If His blood is sufficient for your salvation, then His blood sufficient to sustain you through every challenge and every sin and every temptation.
Jesus is enough.

    You don't have to be something you're not. It doesn't matter if the whole world doesn't understand you or judges you. He understands. He already sees you. Not the mask you wear for the rest of the world. He sees behind it. He sees you, and He loves you. He took your place so you could be you.

    Your birth certificate and gravestone will both have your name on it, and they'll bookend your life. But someone else wrote your name on those. Only you can write your name on the life that is lived in between.

    I never fulfilled my plan. I never became George. If I had, my life would've been a failure. When I die, I won't be asked why I wasn't Moses or David or George. I'll be asked why I wasn't me.

    I'm going to be who God made me to be. I'm going to be who the world needs. I'm going to be me.

God's love Action Challenge
- What have you been carrying that you need to give over to Christ?

<u>Lifestyle change:</u>

Christian means to be a follower of Christ. That is our ultimate goal: to be Christ-like.

Jesus says, "I am the way and the truth and the life."
- John 14:6

This book opened with lyrics from "Truth be Told" by Matthew West. It said, "Truth be told, the truth is rarely told." The truth is we want to be Christ-like, and Christ is the truth. Because of shame, so few of us live in the truth. We want to be Christ-like, but we're not. We fail all the time. And Satan uses our expectations of ourselves to let shame seep in.

So we constantly question ourselves—Am I enough?

You are the light of the world. A town built on a hill cannot be hidden.
- Matthew 5:14

In a world that is so often fake, if we're going to be the light, we have to live in the truth. We waste so much time on useless "church" things. The truth IS NOT:
- Do I look the way I'm supposed to look?
- Do I sound the way I'm supposed to sound?
- Am I perfect?

You're going to mess up. And God's going to love you anyway. If you didn't then you wouldn't need God or His forgiveness. Christ's sacrifice on the cross would mean nothing. We don't have to hide our faults and the fact that we are human.

He doesn't love me because I'm special. He loves me because He just loves. He helped me so He will help you. He will help you so He will help the ones you love.

Redemption was the 1st-century term used for the price paid to gain the freedom of a slave. I was a slave to shame, guilt, and sin. Christ paid the price to free me of my slavery. He paid your price too. The challenge for you today is to live in this truth. Stop trying to carry the weight of the world. The price is already paid. It's your choice whether you are going to give it to Him.

Today, do as Christ did. Don't open the doors of the church and invite the lost in. Open the door and take the Church out of the building. Go out into the world. Share love with the people who need it. It's not about showing them that you're different. It's about showing that we're all the same. The problems the world is dealing with, I deal with them too. So do you. We aren't spared pain and hardship. I am you and you are me. We are them. We are all one.

Today, live your life in the acceptance that God loves you as much on your worst days as He does on your best. When you accept that, the world can too.

Lesson 22: redemption is real (and it only cost everything).

Dear God
I've been trying awful hard to make You proud of me
But it seems the harder that I try, the harder it becomes
And I feel like giving up most of the time
Dear God
I've been chasing their approval and it's killin' me
And I know the more I try to prove, the less I have to show
And I'm stuck inside my head most of the time
But if I pray a little harder, If I follow all the rules
I wonder, could I ever be enough?
'Cause I try and try just to fall back down again
And I ask myself why do I try to chase the wind?
I should lean into the mystery
Maybe hope is found in a melody
So I wanna try again. Oh, I'm gonna try again
And dear child
I hope you know how much I love you and I'm proud of you
And please believe
The thoughts I have for you will never change or fade away
And when you felt like giving up, I never did
'Cause I'm not scared of imperfections
Or the questions in your head
Just know that you have always been enough
'Cause you tried and you tried
And I saw you wrestle with every how, every why
I was right there listening
So just fall into the mystery
And I'll meet you here in the melody
Try, just to try again
Oh, child would you try again?
My child, you can love again

- *"Dear God" by Cory Asbury*

The first few times I heard this song I cried and cried. It's my life. You've read two books to hear it all, but you could've just listened to this song.

Hearing this song, for one of the first times in my life, I felt like somebody understood. Someone else was expressing what it felt like to be me. In the end, I guess that's what we all need: to be understood. To know that through all the chaos—all the ups and downs—we are not alone.

After a few listens (when I could get through the song without sobbing the whole time) it struck me that it was a letter to God. It struck me that there has always been someone who understood what it felt like to be me.

He has always known. He knew me before I was ever created. He knows the number of hairs on my head. I am not alone. I have never been alone. During failure. During mental health struggles. During divorce. During addiction. I was never alone.

You are never alone.

I struggle to pray. I've always felt guilty about that. People ask me to pray for them. I try to, but I don't feel like it's going anywhere. Maybe deep down I still don't feel worthy of Him hearing me.

But, then again, maybe that was His plan all along. That I would struggle for so long to talk to Him that one day I'd decide to write for Him instead. I thought these books were for George. I thought they were intended for the world to know about the man who shaped my life. These books were meant to be my chance to say all the things to you that I failed to say to him.

But as I write this ending, I realize he wasn't the target audience. Neither were you. God was. These books have been my prayer to God. They were all the things I've wanted to say to Him but never felt worthy of saying. They're my admission of who I am without Him and my acknowledgement of His power over my life.

God, I have trouble talking to You. It makes me feel guilty and ashamed, but it's true. But I can write for You. I can live for You. I won't mourn the gifts You've chosen not to give me. Instead, I'll celebrate the ones You have.

This last lesson is to You. That is my redemption. Your love redeemed me. It bought back my life. When You hung on that cross, You didn't just pay for my sin. You paid for my shame too. I don't have to be more. I don't have to be enough. I don't have to write the perfect ending to a book. I just have to talk to you. Be with You. Worship You. Love You.

So, I'll end the book the same way I wrote it: talking to You. But this time I'll do it knowingly and directly. I'm not ending the book this way because I believe it is the best way to do so. I'm doing it because it's the truth. In the end, that's all that matters. To live in the truth. In a book series based in the truth, here are the most true words I'll ever write.

Dear God,

    I tried awful hard to make you proud of me. Been trying my whole life actually. For a long time, that's all I thought I had to give the world: effort. To try. But the harder I tried, the harder it became.

    So I just tried again. I tried harder because I had to. I prayed harder because I had to.

    But I felt like giving up most of the time. I spent my life not chasing their approval but chasing my own. This was an approval I was never able to receive. I couldn't receive it because I resolved to never give it. It was a resolution I made while standing beside a bed in St. Joseph's Hospital in Lexington, Kentucky on July 14th, 2004. I was seeking my approval, and it almost killed me.

    I'm stuck inside my head most of the time. To this day, and probably for every day that I'll live, I'm stuck in my head. I didn't deserve George. I didn't deserve Georgia. But most of all, I didn't deserve You. But maybe if I tried a little harder? Maybe if I followed all the rules? Maybe if I was perfect? Maybe then I'd be enough.

    Maybe hope would be found in the next self-help book that I read in secret. So I read again. Maybe hope would be found in the next race I ran. Or the next weight I lifted. Or the next award I won. Or the next compliment I received. Or anywhere. Somewhere. Maybe hope was out there. So I looked and looked and looked. I tried and tried and tried.

    But one day in Peru I saw myself in a little girl. I saw a little girl who isn't perfect but who was going to grow up trying to be. A little girl who could do it because her daddy could do it. A little girl who already couldn't have pink days. A little girl who was me but deserved to be more than me. Georgia was my child, so I tried again. When everything in me knew it was useless to try because I could never be enough, Georgia was still my child. So I tried again.

    For thirteen years, I gave up nearly every single day. I gave up on faith. I gave up on hope. I gave up on love. But then I'd ask myself, "Would Bubby be proud of me?"

    And I'd drag myself back up and keep going. Not for me but for him. Not out of hope that things could get better but with the certainty that they never would. I couldn't give him a life he'd be proud of, but I could get back up again.

All those years ago, he told me he thought I may strike out, but he never thought I'd go down looking. So I didn't. I struck out over and over in life, but I refused to go down looking. I fought back against depression, darkness, and addiction. Still, I fought out of my duty to honor George and my resolve to never quit. Not because I got to but because I had to.

So I kept trying. But this time I didn't try alone. I tried with Sarah. You used Sarah's love to remind me of Yours. You sent her to me when I was a broken man—losing my license because of a DUI, a recovering alcoholic, refusing to even try to recover from problems that ran much deeper than alcohol.

But she loved me anyway. Not at first as a husband but as a person. As a human being who deserved love just because he was a human being. She loved the shell of me enough that I thought maybe she could love the darkness hiding inside too. So I stopped trying and I leaned into the mystery.

So I'll pray a little harder. But not because I have to. I'll pray a little harder because I want to have a relationship with You. I'll try a little harder because You deserve for me to try. I'll read a little harder because I want to know more about You. I'll try to follow all the rules because I want to honor the sacrifice You made for me.

Finally, I can accept the truth. I'm Your child. I know You love me, and You're proud of me. Not proud of who I want to be or who I worked so hard to become, but of who I am. I know the thoughts and feelings You have for me will never change.

All those days I gave up, You never did. You stayed hanging there on the cross. During those six hours that felt like an eternity, You looked out over time and saw me give up again and again and again. You saw me get back up only to fall again and again and again. But You never gave up on me.

You saw me try and try. You saw me wrestle with every how and every why. Through it all, You were right there with me. So I'll just fall into Your mystery. I'll accept the unknown. My mistakes aren't over. They've probably only just begun. But when I fall, I'm still Your child.

I'll meet You someday. And George will be at the gates to introduce me to You. And you'll both tell me how proud you are of me. Maybe one day I'll be able to be proud of myself. But until then, I'm Your child. So no matter how many times I fall, I'll try just to try again. I'm Your child, so I'll love again. I'm Your child, so today and forever more, I love again.

And lastly, God, I'll do what I should do first but usually fail to do. I'll do what I want to spend the rest of my life doing. I want to thank You. Thank You God for giving me parents who showed me the way to You.

Thank You God for giving me an uncle who was more than a brother. Thank You God for giving me a daughter who reminded me life was worth fighting for. Thank You God for giving me a wife who reminded me of Your love and that I was enough to accept it. Thank You God for giving me a brother who I can call my best friend. But, most of all, Thank You God for me. Amen.

Love,

Your child

Redemption Life Challenge

3. Then Jesus told them this parable: 4. "Suppose one of you has a hundred sheep and loses one of them. Doesn't he leave the ninety-nine in the open country and go after the lost sheep until he finds it? 5. And when he finds it, he joyfully puts it on his shoulders 6. and goes home. Then he calls his friends and neighbors together and says, 'Rejoice with me; I have found my lost sheep.' 7. I tell you that in the same way there will be more rejoicing in heaven over one sinner who repents than over ninety-nine righteous persons who do not need to repent.
- Luke 15:3-7

Love is Real and *Love Redeems* have told my story. I only have Georgia half of the time, but during those days she gets all of me. She gets to know who her Daddy really is. Not the shell of myself I had become. I have my wife Sarah who is my inspiration in everything.

I was the lost lamb. I did everything wrong. But God left the 99 for me.

Like I told Sarah on our wedding day, I'm done trying to be a better man. I'm done trying to be George or Dad. I'm ready to be me.

I always asked myself, "Would Bubby be proud of me?" That's how I kept going for so long. That one question. I always knew the answer was no, but I refused to give up until it was yes. I believe the answer has finally changed.

On my good days, I'm going to be me. And on my bad ones, I'm still going to be me. And Bubby will be proud of me. Because I'm me. I'm going to love myself on my red days just as much as I do on my purple ones because God does.

Like in *Love is Real*, this last challenge isn't a one-off thing. It's a challenge for the rest of your life. You cannot be tried for a case that is no longer on the docket. You don't have to be enough to overcome your sins because they have already been overcome. You're not just redeemed today, but forever more.

Redemption doesn't mean you're going to be perfect. It doesn't mean you're never going to make a mistake. It means those mistakes do not define you. They do not have to be hidden. Embrace them. Highlight them even.

> *If I'm not dead, You're not done*
> *Greater things are still to come*
> *Oh I believe*
> *This is my testimony*
> *From death to life*
> *Cause grace rewrote my story, I'll testify*
> *By Jesus Christ the Righteous*
> *I'm justified*
> *This is my testimony*
> *- "My Testimony" by Elevation Worship*

This has been my story. It isn't yours. Hopefully somebody out there needed to hear my story. But maybe what they really needed was to hear yours. Maybe my story was just meant to give you the push to tell yours. Tell your story to the world. Tell it with your whole heart. You're not dead, so He's not done. Greater things are still to come.

> *I'll never know how much it cost*
> *To see my sin upon that cross*
> *- "Here I Am to Worship" by Hillsong Worship*

I'm not sure we'll ever truly know how much it cost for our sin to be placed on the cross. It cost a sinless man to take on all sin. It cost the King of all Kings to be mocked, beaten, humiliated, spit on, murdered. It cost a Father His Son. It cost it all. It cost everything. And that price was paid for you.

Redeem means to buy back. That's what He did. He bought back your life—your faith, your hope, your peace, your joy, your love. And the cost was everything. He paid that price because that's what you're worth to Him: everything.

The answer for your life and for paying back His sacrifice isn't found in you defeating whatever problems you're dealing with. In my refusal to give up, I fought to overcome my inadequacies. But the need to be more became a sickness. Don't replace one sickness with another. Don't become consumed with being more.

I was given George's Bible when he died. In it, I found a bookmark. Here it is in the book I was reading while writing this one. (The book is *Man's Search for Meaning* by Viktor E. Frankl.)

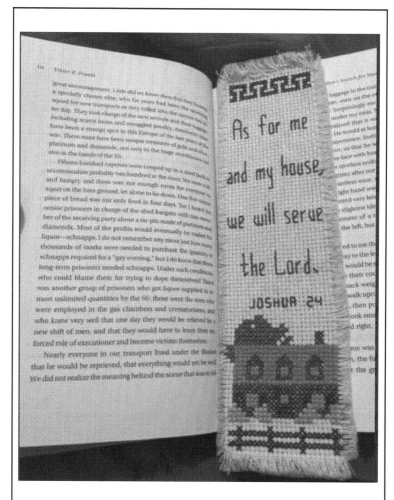

In *Love is Real*, I shared that I started reading self-help books once I knew I was going to have a daughter. I was trying to fix myself through sheer willpower and determination. If the answer was in the world, I was going to find it. And all that time, saving my place in book after book after book, was this bookmark. Through all those years of running from my shame—of running from God—this bookmark was there. When I was running from the last thing George ever said to me—If you ever want to see me again, you have to get back in church—this bookmark was there. When I opened all those books in the early morning hours so no one else would know, I would see this bookmark. Thousands of times, I've picked up this bookmark and put it to the side so I could find my answer in one book or another. Find the cure that would make all my struggles go away.

What I couldn't accept while I poured through book after book but never felt any different was that I didn't have to do all of that. All those years of looking to George, I was looking past the truth he had left behind for me. I was picking up the answer every day and setting it to the side.

The answer wasn't in my work ethic. It wasn't in my grit. It wasn't George's life that was ultimately my compass toward the truth; it was his death. I didn't have to read all those books. I just had to read the bookmark: "As for me and my house, we will serve the Lord."

That's where I found my redemption, and it is where you can find yours. Your answer isn't in *Love is Real*. It isn't in *Love Redeems*. It won't be in *Love > ___* either. It's in this bookmark. Your redemption lies in that one choice. It doesn't matter who you've been or the mistakes you've made.

The answer for your life and paying back His sacrifice is to stop trying to pay it back at all. You can't. Your life cost everything. And everything was given freely. It was given freely because God is love.

So instead of trying to pay it back, just accept it. Accept the free gift. As for you and your house, serve the Lord. Serve God because God is love. And love redeems.

Part 5: Appendix

A personal invitation

God gave me a second chance at life. I want to spend the rest of my life helping others find their second chance too. Alan and I created Love is Real Wellness to help those in recovery live better and love more. Join us and the Love is Real Community for daily support.

- Visit Loveisrealwellness.com. Go to the "Work with Adam" tab to learn more about my 20-week *Live Better, Love More Program*. Quite frankly, it is the most effective and scientifically backed holistic wellness program available.
- Subscribe to "Love is Real Wellness" on Youtube for daily "A Real Minute" videos
- Follow us at facebook.com/loveisrealwellness

Testimonials

Adam helped me grow as a person and learn what it means to love myself. I held myself to this impossible standard and couldn't shake the feeling that what I was doing wasn't enough. Sometimes all we need is for someone to show us what we can't see for ourselves. And Adam did that for me. Adam loved me when I couldn't love myself. I am truly grateful for the impact he has had on my life.

-Rachel Hughes
Lexington, KY

Having the session with Adam helped me go from a reactive mindset to a proactive mindset. As a result, I took forward steps to broaden my network in order to get my dream job! It was a really enjoyable experience. I recommend him to anyone wanting to make a positive change in their lives.
-Kelly Dugan
Atlanta, Georgia

I believe in what Adam was telling me and have tried to incorporate it into my everyday life. I am still not perfect and don't expect to ever get there. But what that hour zoom meeting with Adam did was give me a step in the right direction. If you are battling mental or physical health, I encourage you to take some time and speak with him.
-John Wemple
Richmond, KY

Bible verses used in Love Redeems

Job 31:1
Psalm 73:26
Ecclesiastes 3:11-12
Isaiah 40:31
Lamentations 3:22
Ezekiel 36:26
Matthew 5:14
Matthew 5:27-28
Matthew 6:25-26
Matthew 6:27
Matthew 6:34
Matthew 9:11-13
Matthew 17:20
Matthew 18:19-20
Luke 3:21-22
Luke 10:38-42
Luke 15:3-7
Luke 23:39-43
John 14:6
John 8:32
John 10:10
John 16:30
Romans 5:1
Romans 7:15
Romans 7:21-25
Romans 10:9
1 Corinthians 9:24-27
1 Corinthians 10:13
2 Corinthians 4:17
Ephesians 1:6-10
Philippians 4:12-13
1 Thessalonians 5:16-18
1 Timothy 1:15-17
2 Timothy 4:7-8
Titus 2:12
Hebrews 8:12
James 4:6
1 Peter 1:24
1 Peter 5:7
2 Peter 3:8-14

Sources

Life Application Bible Study Guide
How to Make Disease Disappear by Dr. Rangan Chatterjee
Uncommon by Tony Dungy
Quiet strength by Tony Dungy
Man's Search For Meaning by Viktor E. Frankl
Not a Fan by Kyle Idleman
The Depression Cure by Dr. Stephen Ilardi
Strong Fathers, Strong Daughters by Meg Meeker
Your God is Too Small by J.B. Phillips
Emotionally Healthy Spirituality by Peter Scazzero
A Grace Disguised by Gerald Lawson Sittser
Darkness Visible by William Styron
A Purpose Driven Life by Rick Warren

Acknowledgements

- Jake Bingham - Editor
- Alan Reid – Co-owner of Love is Real Wellness
- Richard Sester - Cover page artwork
- Hunter West and Maryssa Miller - Junior Editors

Made in the USA
Columbia, SC
04 January 2025